THE WORRYWART'S PRAYER BOOK

The Worrywart's Prayer Book

40 "Help-Me-Get-a-Grip God" Meditations and Prayers

Allia Zobel-Nolan

Health Communications, Inc.
Deerfield Beach, Florida

www.hcibooks.com

Library of Congress Cataloging-in-Publication Data is available from the Library of Congress.

©2006 Allia Zobel-Nolan
ISBN 0-7573-0260-2

Publisher: Faith Communications, Inc.
An Imprint of Health Communications, Inc.
3201 S.W. 15th Street
Deerfield Beach, FL 33442-8190

Cover design by Larissa Hise Henoch
Cover artwork by Mary Pat Pino
Inside book design by Lawna Patterson Oldfield

For the glory of God,

who gave me this book to write

so I can refer to it often, and for my husband,

Desmond Finbarr Nolan, whose patience, love,

fortitude and support surrounded

me while I wrote it.

CONTENTS

Acknowledgments ix

Introduction xi

1   Get Ready, Get Set . . . Worry...1

2   Your Worries? Or Mine? 5

3   Relaxing Without Guilt 9

4   Ten Pounds of Flesh 15

5   Minding Today's Business 19

6   Fortuitous Failure 25

7   I Hate Traveling, but I Love Having Traveled 31

8   Chasing After Time 35

9   What People Say—What People Think 39

10 Finding a Mate 43

11 Job Jitters 49

12 Fueling Anxiety with Negativity 53

13 Neat to a Fault 59

14 Who Stole My Body? 65

15 Accepting Joy 71

16 Loss 77

17 Change—The Worrywart's Friend 83

18 Don't Worry, Be Silly..89

19 Possessive Possessions 95

20 Timing 101

21 A Sympathetic Ear 107

22 Limiting Others' Lives 113

23 Angels Abounding 119

24 Attitude of Gratitude 125

25 Prayer, Practice, Pretending 131

26 Real Success 137

27 Evil 143

28 Your Father Always Loves You 149

29 Reining In Imagination 153

30 Two Worrisome Words...159

31 What's Done Is Done...165

32 Criticism..171

33 Terrorism...177

34 Can You Hear Me Now? (Being Alone)................183

35 Life—What a Pain 189

36 God Is My Sleeping Pill...197

37 Testing 1, 2, 3 203

38 Addicted to Worry..209

39 Death: The Ultimate Worry 215

40 It's Only Money...221

Notes 227

ACKNOWLEDGMENTS

Thanks and blessings to the many people who believed in this book, including: my let-there-be-no-crisis-before-its-time husband, Desmond Finbarr Nolan; the woman who taught me the fine art of worrying, my mother, Lucille; my laugh-on-the-outside-worry-on-the-inside dad, Alvin; my yoga-loving, full-of-patience-and-love sister, Vicky; my easygoing grandfather, Louis Frank; my agent and friend, Rita Rosenkranz; my closest friends, Sheila Papaleo, Patricia Haggerty, Mary Pat Pino and Joyce Giordano; my editor, Amy Hughes; and my associates Natalie Provenzano-Brodie, Candy Warren, Phyllis Schreiber, Alison Munoz, Else Sonn, Christine Guido and Wendy Bocuzzi, who listened and listened some more. Thank you also to my three feline angels, Sinead, Angela and McDuff, who could teach us all a thing or two about not worrying.

INTRODUCTION

I, at any rate, am convinced that God is not playing at dice.

—ALBERT EINSTEIN

H i, I'm Allia Nolan, and I'm a worrywart. I've been one all my life. In fact for me, worrying *is* my life. From the time I put my foot out of the bed (will my big toe find the thumbtack I lost last week?) to the moment I lay my head on the pillow (will the killer bees I saw on the eleven o'clock news make it to my door by morning?), I'm a nervous wreck. I fall asleep worrying whether I will, and have dreams of not waking up until I do.

Sometimes it's big things, like earthquakes, nuclear annihilation, meteorites, eclipses, aliens and bridge collapses (and now terrorism), that have me chewing my nails. Sometimes it's the usual concerns, like lightning, airplanes, the ozone layer, elevators, reengineering, West Nile virus and the return of polyester. But mostly, it's harmless everyday situations I blow totally out of proportion. A little indigestion? Food poisoning. Wrong number? A robber's casing my house. Summer storm? A tornado for sure. And that's just a drop in the sea of my jitters.

I obsess over irons and candles and other things that need to be turned off, put out, opened, closed, switched on, filled up and emptied. I worry about dust mites, radon, electromagnetic waves and that too many leaves falling on the same spot on my new car could cause a dent. I'm anxious for family, friends, relatives, strangers, world leaders and TV personalities. I'm concerned for mankind in general, even lawyers. I fret about the past. The present. The pluperfect.

But it gets worse. I'm a Christian.

So where's God while I'm wringing my hands? Probably in his office, with a "Don't worry. Be happy." sign on his desk. I can see him now, sitting there, shaking his head. And while I can't be certain, I can guess what he's thinking. *What is wrong with this woman? She calls herself a Christian? Where's her faith? Where's her trust? Doesn't she realize I'm in charge? Doesn't she know all the worrying in the world—even by a professional like her—is moot? Haven't I told her over and over, "Do not be afraid"? Didn't my Son explain about the lilies, the birds of the field, the rock and the bread, the snake and the fish? What gives? What do I have to do to make her understand?*

Well, God knows, I'm a little slow. And frankly, I've been out of the loop for a while now. (I'm a prodigal recently returned.) So it took me longer than most before the light went on. But when it did, I finally realized who calls the shots. Even better, it dawned on me that anytime I wanted to, with God's grace, I could quit being a Nervous Nellie and start enjoying this wonderful life he's given me. So that's what I'm doing. And this book is part of the process. I wrote it to help me worry less and trust God more. It's full of prayers and affirmations I use (and you can, too) as my faith-strengthening regimen.

Remember, though, like any training program, we can't do it once, forget it and expect results. It takes dedication. But will I worry about it? Will I make myself anxious? With God's help, I think not. Enjoy.

CHAPTER 1

Get Ready, Get Set... Worry

To me, faith means not worrying.

—JOHN DEWEY

Blessed is the person who's too busy to worry in the daytime and too tired to worry at night.

—EARL RINEY

We are always getting ready to live, but never living.

—RALPH WALDO EMERSON

All worry is atheism, because it is a want of trust in God.

—BISHOP FULTON J. SHEEN

Banish anxiety from your heart.

—ECCLESIASTES 11:10

In actual life every great enterprise begins with
and takes its first forward step in faith.

—AUGUST WILHELM VON SCHLEGEL

Do you get in a tizzy about beginning things—a course, commitment, maybe even a chocolate layer cake? It's a common worrywart trap. I ought to know. This book's a perfect example. First I talked about it for months. Then I worried over whether I'd have enough time to write it. Then, of course, it was, would the right words come? Could I fill a whole book? Would it be any good? Yadda, yadda, yadda. Okay, maybe I was using my anxieties as a form of procrastination. But anyway you look at it, I expended a lot of energy for nothing.

What's wrong with this picture? I forgot about God. And it was only after I put my worrying aside long enough to ask for his help that I was able to get the lead out. It was then I came to realize I needed to make a move—or move on. How many of us can afford to waste time with nothing to show for it? If we put the time it takes to worry to another use—writing, cooking or beginning something—at least we'll have something tangible, good or bad, to show for ourselves. And surely, a sense of accomplishment feels a whole lot better than a headful of empty anxieties.

PRAYER

Today, Lord, I will remember to look to you first and foremost before I start anything. Let me trust your plans for me. Let me anticipate new beginnings—the way I'd imagine you'd want me to—as a child looks forward to a birthday gift. And, Lord, once I do get started, let me trust that you have my very best interests at heart, whatever the outcome, even if it's not what I expected.

♦ ♦ ♦

CHAPTER 2

Your Worries? Or Mine?

[T]ake captive every thought to make it obedient to Christ.

—2 CORINTHIANS 10:5

Brothers, each man, as responsible to God, should remain
in the situation God called him to.

—1 CORINTHIANS 7:24

One cannot weep for the entire world.
It is beyond human strength. One must choose.

—JEAN ANNOUILH

Undoubtedly, we become what we envisage.

—CLAUDE M. BRISTOL

Nobody's born a worrywart. Babies don't spend large portions of their days anxiety-ridden. They have an innate trust everything will turn out hunky-dory. And, for the most part, it does. It isn't until children learn from parents, relatives and society that there are things "out there" they should be concerned about, that the world becomes a very scary place.

Case in point: a woman named Katie remembers being taken on an elevator for the first time with her dad when she was seven. "It was like going on an amusement park ride," she recalls. "I loved the feeling." That is, until one day she went with a friend and her mother to Macy's. "I asked if we could take the elevator," Katie says. "But my friend's mother whisked us toward the stairs. As we went, I felt her hand go all clammy. And when I asked why we were walking up, I remember she said, "Elevators aren't safe, Katie. They can fall." After that, Katie confesses, riding an elevator was never the same.

Worrywarts soak up other people's worries like a dry sponge on a wet countertop. We have plenty of our own. Yet we continue to compound our lives by taking on our friends', relatives', even perfect strangers' anxieties as well. It's almost as though if we're not worrying, we're not happy. We get caught up in the act without thinking, without taking time to examine and reassess what we're doing. It's like obsessing that our dogs will run into the street and get run over because the neighbor does—then realizing we don't even own a dog.

Getting anxious over something because someone else does won't help them or us. Staying peaceful, then asking God to help us separate the other person's issues from our own, will. This isn't callous or uncaring. It's what we need to do to keep from being in constant turmoil. We can certainly empathize with others who are worrying (we know how unsettling it feels) and pray they find peace. But the next step is letting go and letting God—detaching and trusting in his plan for them. Sometimes the mere act of not reacting (which for us worrywarts takes a lot of doing) can be a good way to show others that being anxious is a choice. We can feel the worry and then hand it over to God. Or strap it on, walk around with it and pass it on to others along our way.

On the other hand, think of the possibilities if we just say "No." For instance, the next time someone says, "Aren't you worried about nuclear war?" we can answer, "Well actually, God's helping me with airplane anxieties at the moment. So why don't I leave nuclear war to you?"

PRAYER

Dear Lord,

  Boy, are you ever patient! Now I'm asking you for help not only to deal with my own worries, but also to stop me from taking on everyone else's. We worrywarts are certainly a handful. Even so, I know you love me. So please, God, help me remember: (1) there's nothing wrong in saying "No" to the negative pull of other people's worries; (2) to detach and trust that your plans for others are unfolding according to design; and (3) that learning to have faith in you can be just as contagious as worrying.

◆ ◆ ◆

CHAPTER 3

Relaxing Without Guilt

Finally, brethren, whatever is true, whatever is honorable, whatever is right, whatever is pure, whatever is lovely, whatever is of good repute, if there is any excellence and if anything worthy of praise, dwell on these things.

—PHILIPPIANS 4:8 NASU

There smiles no Paradise on earth so fair
But guilt will raise avenging phantoms there.

—FELICIA D. HUMANS

By the seventh day, God had finished the work he
had been doing; so on the seventh day he rested.

—GENESIS 2:2

Come to me all you who are weary and burdened,
and I will give you rest.

—MATTHEW 11:28

My people will live in peaceful dwelling places,
in secure homes, in undisturbed places of rest.

—ISAIAH 32:18

Take rest; a field that has rested gives a bountiful crop.

—OVID

Gillian draws her bath. She pours in a capful of lavender bath petals and stares as they melt in the water. She lights a perfumed candle and inhales the sweet fragrance. Strains of Enya echo softly from her bedroom stereo. Her two cats lie nestled close to one other, their eyes half closed, purring in contentment. Finally, when the atmosphere seems just perfect, she slips into the tub and lets out a sigh of pleasure. You can almost hear her muscles relax. She closes her eyes and lets the day's worries float away. . . .

NOT! Well, okay, maybe for a second. But then instead of relaxing and enjoying a well-deserved respite, Gillian's mind starts fussing with a dozen annoying trivialities. First she gives in to silly doubts. *Did I turn the oven off? Did I lock the door? Was this the night I was supposed to meet Gwen for dinner?* Then the brass section—the replay of work anxieties—brings up the rear. *Yikes! My expense account! Isn't the cutoff tomorrow? But I'm in meetings all day tomorrow. I'll have to go in early—at least 5:00 A.M. So what am I sitting here like a dolt for? I'd better get out of this bath and into bed, fast.* And before you can say "Gillian is a worrywart," her quiet time and her plans to detox from the day go swirling, like the water, down the drain.

Sound familiar? Join the club. According to the late Dale Carnegie, author and admitted worrier, we're at our most vulnerable after hours, when we're trying to wind down from work. Why? Carnegie says when our minds aren't busy, they become a magnet for emotions, such as worry, fear, hate, jealousy and envy. "Such emotions," he explains, "are so violent they tend to drive out of our minds all peaceful and happy thoughts."

Unless we learn to stop them—nip them in the bud before they get the chance to ruin our baths or the quiet time we spend reading a book. God believes in relaxation. He himself kicked back after a full week of creation. So surely he never meant us to feel guilty about indulging in a little R & R. Jesus knew the importance of downtime. At the height of his ministry, the Bible tells us, when he was being besieged by the poor, the sick and the lame, so much so, that he and the disciples didn't even have a chance to eat, he took some of them aside and said, "Come with me . . . to a quiet place and get some rest." And that's what Jesus offers us poor, bedraggled worrywarts—some rest. If we can only hold our negative emotions at bay long enough to receive it.

So the next time we're soaking away our worries and Satan's helpers start stirring things up in our brains, refuse them up front. Saying something out loud, for instance, "Stop!" or "Go away!" or "God grant me serenity" or even "Scram" calls our attention to the intruder, so we can switch him right off. Then we can turn our thoughts back to relaxing while we thank God for the wonderful gifts he's given us—hot water, fragrant candles, calming music, rainbows in the bubbles and, oh yes, those lazy—ah—peaceful balls of fluff, our cats, who never have a problem with relaxing and never have worried a day in their furry lives.

The good news is that while we're thanking God for these blessings, we're immersing ourselves in the present, receiving all the good things—and relaxation is one of them—God wants to give us. The trick here is to work as hard at relaxing as we do at worrying.

PRAYER

Dear God,

When it comes to relaxing, I know I'm my own worst enemy. I constantly undermine perfectly peaceful times with trifles. I can stop. But I can't do it without you. I pray you'll help me expect and accept good things from you, as I would from a doting parent, without always sabotaging my joy. Help me to find peace in the fact that it gives you joy to see me happy, and that I can always find my rest in you.

◆ ◆ ◆

CHAPTER 4

Ten Pounds of Flesh

A really busy person never knows how much he weighs.

—EDGAR WATSON HOWE

Man looks at the outward appearance, but
the LORD looks at the heart.

—1 SAMUEL 16:7

I praise you because I am fearfully and wonderfully
made. . . . My frame was not hidden from you
when I was made.

—PSALM 139:14, 15

Stop judging by mere appearances.

—JOHN 7:24

Your beauty should . . . be that of your inner self,
the unfading beauty of a gentle and quiet spirit, which
is of great worth in God's sight. For this is the way
the holy women . . . who put their hope in God used
to make themselves beautiful.

—1 PETER 3:3

If Jesus were to give his Sermon on the Mount today, he just might change the wording to something like "I say to you, do not worry about what you shall eat, what you shall drink, what you shall wear . . . or how much you weigh." Too bad words like these would fly right over most worrywarts' heads. We'd be too busy asking our friends, "Does this (size 8) dress make me look huge?" or "Aren't I a total elephant in these pants?"

And we're not talking the seriously obese here. We're talking worrywarts like you and me who've bought into a popular notion that thin is in and any woman who doesn't stay 115 pounds (eight pounds more if she's pregnant) either by means of womb-to-tomb dieting and/or compulsive exercising is an undisciplined *gordo* destined to get larger every year until she can't even fit through the door of her own house.

Whew! With thoughts like this, no wonder we have agita. And let's face it, it's all a ruse. Our oh-my-gosh-we're-turning-into-a-blimp worries signal not so much a weight problem as an image problem. We look in the mirror and we're not satisfied. We don't like what we see. We don't like how we feel. We consider ourselves failures because we don't measure up to some unrealistic standard of beauty that Seventh Avenue sets. Still, we were thin(ner) once. We could do it again. Maybe if we cut out the cake and bagels, or buy one of those abs belts . . .

On the other hand, we could face the mirror, smooth down our dresses and ask God to remind us we're made in his image, not Hollywood's. Then instead of getting antsy over this bulge or that, we could see ourselves as God made us—amazing creatures, every one different, with a body that can walk, talk, think, feel and make choices. And while we're at it, why not look ourselves in the eye and ask questions like, "Will God stop loving me because I've gone up a dress size?" or "If I were ten pounds thinner, would I be a better person in God eyes?" Answering these questions with a resounding "Nah!" will bolster our ailing images so that we can begin loving the person we see for who she/he is—not for how much she/he weighs.

PRAYER

Lord, help me let the air out of my ingrained notion of myself as a blimp. Build in me a new improved image that focuses, like you do, on what's in my heart, not what's on my hips. Show me how silly and vain I am when I let something as insignificant as ten pounds (the same pounds I keep losing and gaining back) have such a powerful effect on me. Give me the strength to stop putting so much emphasis on my appearance, to accept and appreciate my body, and to thank you for making me in your image. Finally, empower me to get my soul in shape, so I can build my identity from the inside out, not the outside in.

◆ ◆ ◆

CHAPTER 5

Minding Today's Business

Let there be no crisis before its time.

—DESMOND FINBARR NOLAN

Now listen, you who say, "Today or tomorrow we will go
to this or that city." . . . Why, you do not even know what
will happen tomorrow. . . . Instead, you ought to say,
"If it is the Lord's will, we will live and do this or that."

—JAMES 4:13, 15

Today is the tomorrow you worried about, and all is well.

—ANONYMOUS

It is when tomorrow's burden is added to the burden of
today that the weight is more than a man can bear. Never
load yourself so. If you find yourself so loaded, at least
remember this: it is your own doing, not God's. He urges
you to *leave the future to Him, and mind the present.*

—GEORGE MACDONALD (EMPHASIS ADDED)

My favorite author, Dr. M. Scott Peck, tells a really great story
in *Further Along the Road Less Traveled* about a rabbi who
refuses to second-guess God's plans for him. Seems the rabbi passes
by a policeman every day at the same time to go to temple, Scott
says. And one day, the officer's in a bad mood, so he grabs hold of
the rabbi and demands to know where he is going. "I don't know,"
says the rabbi. "What do you mean you don't know? You go to
temple every day at this time," the policeman yells. "So why are you
telling me you don't know?" and with that, the policeman hauls
the rabbi off to jail for trying to play him a fool. On the way there,
the rabbi says to the policeman, "You asked me where I was going
and, see, I told you. I just don't know."

No matter how predictable things look or, for that matter, how
worrisome they appear, from minute to minute, hour to hour, like
the rabbi, we really "just don't know" what will happen. This is why
a saying my husband coined is so on the mark: "Let there be no crisis before its time," he constantly tells me. It's his way of reminding

me how senseless it is to time-travel into the future to try to resolve problems that haven't even occurred yet. I hate to say this (and mind you, it doesn't happen very often), but I have to admit, he's 100 percent correct.

Being anxious about tomorrow's problems is a habit worrywarts are famous for. It's a chronic need to be ready, prepared and have contingency plans for every eventuality that, in and of itself, is totally impossible. If there's a nor'easter expected next week, we can make sure we have enough candles and batteries, and maybe buy some extra food in case we lose power. But worrying about what will happen if a tree falls on the house (highly unlikely) or if the wind blows out a window (even more highly unlikely) is really a monumental waste of time. It's like fretting about fixing something before we even know that it's broken.

When a bout of this type of worry comes upon us, our thought patterns run in circles, and like a dog chasing its own tail, we proceed to go over every possible scenario and how we would handle each. Mind you, we've already assumed the calamity will, in fact, happen. So we feel compelled to sift through solutions that will help us manage the ordeal. *What if this happens?* we think. *Well then, we can do this. But then, what if that happens? Okay then, we'll do that. Yeah, but what if this and that both happen? Well then, we'll do this, and then we'll do that.* Problem solving like this makes us feel we're ready for anything, in control, which, of course, makes us feel better. But we can stay stuck in this quagmire for hours, even days, only to find out later, when God's plan unfolds, that there is no crisis at all. Or maybe we find out there is a problem, but it's far from a crisis, and God has already equipped us with the ammunition we need to handle it just fine. Or maybe the problem does turn out to be a crisis, but it's one that God deems necessary, because, in the long run, it will prove to be a lesson that will help us in the future.

Uh-oh—we're doing it again—trying to read God's mind. Small wonder he doesn't drop a Bible on our heads opened to Matthew 6:34 with a huge sticky note posted on top that reads: "You're getting upset for nothing. Have faith. Don't burden yourself. Leave things to me. Read again what my Son told you: 'Don't worry about tomorrow. You've enough on your plate today. Remember, tomorrow's my business. Today is yours.'"

Then maybe we'd learn to trust God, his plan and ourselves, secure in the knowledge that he cares about us and would never give us more than we can handle. Maybe then we'd also learn to take each day as it comes, as a gift, filled with wonderful surprises that would be a shame not to enjoy because we're too busy being anxious about a crisis that will never materialize.

On the other hand, since that's not God's style, maybe we ought to open our Bibles ourselves, read Jesus's words again and write out some stickies of our own. Leave them all over the place—at work, at home, in the car. They could read: "Me—Today; God—Tomorrow" or anything else that will remind us to concentrate on one day at a time. In this way, we can do a good job today (which experts say is the best way to prepare for tomorrow anyway), keep our strength for real crises and let God take care of the rest.

PRAYER

Dearest Jesus,

I know you want us to live in the present. You said so your-self. That's why you give us one day at a time: to learn what we need to learn today, so we can live better tomorrow. But I'm missing the lessons you tuck in each minute when my mind's off in the future creating problems that aren't there and probably won't materialize. So please, Lord, give me the faith to trust you more. Help me look back at all the yesterdays that have turned out so perfectly and see, in spite of my getting upset, that they couldn't have been woven into the tapestry of my life any better. Get me in the habit of concentrating on the business at hand— today's business, so I can enjoy each moment and look to it as another opportunity to do your will.

◆ ◆ ◆

CHAPTER 6

Fortuitous Failure

Every time trouble comes, consider that through it
the Lord is giving you a needed lesson.

—PARAMAHANSA YOGANANDA

But God teaches men through suffering and
uses distress to open their eyes.

—JOB 36:15 TEV

Being humble involves the willingness to be reckoned
a failure in everyone's sight but God's.

—ROY M. PEARSON

Failure is success if we learn from it.

—MALCOLM S. FORBES

Disappointment to a noble soul is what cold water
means to burning metal; it strengthens, tempers,
intensifies, but never destroys it.

—ELIZA TABOR

For all have sinned and fall short of the glory of God.

—ROMANS 3:23

I haven't failed. I've found 10,000 ways that don't work.

—THOMAS EDISON

It is difficulties that show what men are.

—EPICTETUS

The Almighty Father will use life's reverses to
move you forward.

—BARBARA JOHNSON

rue or false: Failure is nothing to worry about. It doesn't just happen to you. It's not the end of the world. We can learn a lot from it. It's not a punishment from God. And it can be, and very often is, the best thing that could ever happen to us.

Those who answered "true" can skip this chapter. Everyone else, grab a highlighter. It's time to learn some failure fundamentals.

For starters, failure brings us closer to God. And anything that nudges us in his direction is nothing to worry about. See, when we're on top of the world, we tend to forget about the Lord. We're too busy whooping it up. Hit a snag, though, and our fingers can't speed-dial him fast enough. The Bible says God sends failure as a reminder to those who've put him on the back burner: "I will abandon my people until they have suffered enough. . . . Perhaps in their suffering they will try to find me," the prophet Hosea writes. And that's exactly what we do. When we have a setback, we turn to God for comfort and answers. "Let's return to the LORD!" Hosea writes. "He has hurt us; but he will be sure to heal us. . . ." That's why it's so important to acknowledge our failures, because then we can go back and receive God's healing grace. On the other hand, God can't help us if we pretend there's nothing wrong. He can't heal us if we never call out to him. Pity those who never own up to failing, or make excuses, or pass the buck, cover up or ignore it. They lose out on their opportunities to let God help. They miss out on his amazing grace.

And don't get anxious thinking failure happens to only you, because failure doesn't play favorites. It happens to everyone. Everyone fails. Not just once, mind you, but over and over again.

The Bible says, "A righteous man may fall seven times and rise again [seven times]." The rest of us might have to quadruple that number. We might not think so—but that's actually a good thing, and here's why: It demonstrates God's relentless power of patience, forgiveness and love. It gives him the opportunity to lend us a hand over and over. And it shows us that God will never abandon us, ever. It also points out that God separates the sin from the sinner. We may have failed, but we're not failures.

Failure is not the end of the world, either. It's not irreversible and never final. Crack open the Good Book and you'll find dozens of people who failed miserably, then went on to become Bible Hall of Famers—people like Abraham, who lied about his wife; Jacob, who stole his brother's birthright; Moses, who murdered and failed to listen to directions; David, who committed adultery and murder; Saul, who failed as a king; Job, who was too righteous; Jonah, who disobeyed a direct order; the disciples, who failed to trust Jesus in a storm and keep awake the night of his betrayal (among other things); Peter, who denied Christ; Thomas, who doubted Jesus; and Paul, who went around murdering Christians. Surely these were grievous mistakes. Yet as soon as these folks admitted they were wrong ("I have sinned against the LORD," said David) and repented (Peter "went out and wept bitterly."), God showered them with remedial grace, after which they put failure behind them, dried themselves off and continued on with the plans God had for them. Indeed, God works with what he has. He never throws the baby out with the bathwater.

Then, too, if we're open to it, we can learn a lot from failure.

Humility, among other things. Because when everything's rosy, and things are going from good to better, we start to overestimate ourselves. A string of successes gets us all puffed out, and we act as though God has nothing to do with our good fortune. We forget that through him all things are possible, but without him, we can't even lift a pinky. So for our own good, God taps us on the shoulder with a little failure as a reminder of who's who. The Bible says, "The Lord will make you go through hard times, but he himself will be there to teach you. . . ." And in this case, what he's teaching us is that hubris and pride don't score high points with him. He much prefers a humble, contrite man. So the lesson going forward is, we might want to try to be less full of ourselves and more full of God.

God also uses failure to teach us patience, motivate us to strive more and help us build endurance, which the Bible tells us "brings God's approval." The Bible also says God uses failure as a test, and that when we get an "A," we can expect good things. "Happy is the person who remains faithful under trials," writes James, "because when he succeeds in passing such a test, he will receive as his reward the life which God has promised. . . ." Job did, and though it was rough going there for a while, he endured, learned a huge lesson about making himself look good at God's expense, then got his health and all his goodies back, with interest. So, far from being a punishment, Job's setback turned out to be a good thing for him. Indeed, a setback reminds us to sit back, take another look at where we're going and perhaps reset our priorities. God often sends it to us as an eye-opener—a warning that we need to reevaluate and redirect our lives. Like Balaam's donkey (in Numbers, chapter 22), failure can be trying to tell us we're either headed in the wrong direction or about to make a big mistake.

Okay, so now that we've gone over a few of the points about failure, let's see if we've revised our opinions. Raise your hands if you agree: failure can and may just be nothing to worry about.

Wow! Talk about fast learners.

PRAYER

Dearest God,

Help me, Lord, to see failure, not as a bad thing, but as part of the plan you've arranged for me. Teach me to look past my own insecurities and find the lesson you want me to learn. Shower me with your grace, so I can acknowledge my mistakes, put them in the past, and get on with my life and the purpose you have in mind for me.

♦   ♦   ♦

CHAPTER 7

I Hate Traveling, but I Love Having Traveled

For my part, I travel not to go anywhere, but to go.
I travel for travel's sake. The great affair is to move.

—ROBERT LOUIS STEVENSON

We make our own plans, but the Lord decides where
we will go.

—EXODUS 33:14 TEV

The LORD said I will go with you. . . .

—PROVERBS 16:9 CEV

He will protect you as you come and go now and forever.

—PSALM 121:8

He protected us on our entire journey.

—JOSHUA 24:17

May the LORD keep watch between you and me
when we are away from each other.

—GENESIS 31:49

Nothing can push a worrywart's buttons more than an impending trip. Travel, for people like us, equals trauma. Why, just the mere thought of what could happen gets us so worked up, it's a wonder we go anywhere at all. Whether it's a short business jaunt to Indiana or a much-awaited trip to the Emerald Isles, we're beset by a host of harpies nagging us with negative "watch outs" and "what ifs." While other travelers daydream of sun and fun, new faces, exotic foods, a change of scenery or just plain getting out of the old routine, we're stuck struggling with a dread that threatens to spoil everything for us and anyone unlucky enough to be along for the ride.

We rattle on over superficial things, like whether we're bringing the right clothes, if the weather will be good or if the car will be in the lot when we return. What's really bugging us are the biggies:

Is there a bomb on the plane? Will I get mugged in the city? Will the bus get into an accident? Of course, if we're traveling by car, whoever's driving (except if it's us) is going too fast, taking too many chances. And that was *before* September 11.

Three little words can help us when we're making ourselves sick like this: "God's in charge." Saying them with an added affirmation, "He's in the driver's seat and knows what he's doing," forces us to relinquish control to the only one who really has it: God. We'll still have sweaty hands and a flip-flop stomach, but centering ourselves in God makes the fear bearable and prevents it from escalating.

And actually, there's the rub. A case of travel jitters isn't really about plane crashes and terrorist attacks. It's about losing control—the control we think we (not God) have over the events that take place in our lives. We forget once we ask God to keep us from harm that what happens next is entirely in his hands. But look at it this way: who would we want at the controls? God, who knows all, or you and I who think we know?

Then, too, just for argument's sake, let's look back. How many times have we gotten a panic attack before a trip only to have the trip turn out to be terrific? Was it our worrying that made it so? Or was a pleasant journey what God intended all along? Fact is, we don't know what God has in store for us. We're not privy to his plans. But one thing we should know, worrying won't affect it a lick.

Traveling is supposed to be fun. And it can be if we ask God to stand by us while we work though our nervousness. Granted, the heebie-jeebies won't disappear overnight. But how will we ever be able to go anywhere without stress if we don't start now?

PRAYER

Hi, God. I'm off on a trip again. So naturally, I'm a bundle of nerves. More so than ever because the world is in such turmoil. Hold my hand so I can make it through safe and sane. Help me remember you're in charge and have everything (even air turbulence) under control. Remind me that no matter where my journey takes me, or what mode of transportation I use, you are always there beside me. Lord, please drive away the negative demons that rob me of the fun and exhilaration of my trip. Calm my fears so I can relax. And let my faith in you make this experience a happy one.

P.S. Oh, and, God, ditto the above when I travel in the car with my husband.

◆　◆　◆

CHAPTER 8

Chasing After Time

The sole purpose of life in time is to gain
merit for life in eternity.

—ST. AUGUSTINE

Many are the plans in a man's heart, but it is
the LORD'S purpose that prevails.

—PROVERBS 19:21

Those who make the worst use of their time,
most complain of its shortness.

—LA BRUYERE

Who of you by worrying can add a single hour to his life?

—MATTHEW 6:27

The time God allots to each one of us is like a precious
tissue which we embroider as we best know how.

—ANATOLE FRANCE

The great soul that sits on the throne of the universe
never was, and never will be, in a hurry.

—JOSIAH GILBERT HOLLAND

Man proposes; God disposes.

—THOMAS À KEMPIS

Worrywarts are like the white rabbit in *Alice in Wonderland*.
We're always checking our watches and coming up short on
time. So our primary directive has become finding ways to restruc-
ture our lives. We want to do more in less time—so we can do even
more in the time we've saved. The Bible tells us, "It is not for us to
know how much time God has us down for." You'd never know it,
though, the way we plan our heads off.

Day-timers and Palm Pilots are our bosom buddies. And the
what-did-we-do-before-it time-saving toy—our cell phone—helps

us gain precious minutes by allowing us to do nine million things (aka multitasking) at the same time. So on an average day, we not only grocery shop, exercise, drive to work, bake a batch of cookies for a church function, fold the laundry and oversee homework, but also do all of this *while* we call Mom to make sure her cold is better, arrange carpools for the kids, cancel our spouses' dentist appointments and refill our blood pressure medicine at the pharmacy. As for God, we squeeze in a quick grace before gulping down yesterday's cold pizza, and then at bedtime, maybe, if we don't fall asleep in the middle of it, a short prayer before we turn out the light.

But the clincher is—on the odd day when we can't face up to this self-imposed Herculean schedule—an annoying voice in our heads badgers us: *What's wrong with you? You're very inefficient. Why can't you catch up? Why don't you ever have enough time?* Now, granted, God wants us to have a full life. But he doesn't want us to be so busy we give ourselves an ulcer.

Clearly, if the amount of things we do in a day has us worrying how we're ever going to get them all done, we need a time-out. That panic button we're pushing is sounding an alarm, and the message the red button's flashing is "overload." When things get this bad, we need to stop, make a list of commitments and prioritize.

We may be amazed—when it's all written down—at how much we really do, and how much of it isn't all that necessary. We might also be ashamed to realize how little time we've allotted for God. That might be the time to take a hard look at our lists and weed out some nonessentials so we can come up with a more realistic, less worrisome schedule that includes more time for prayer, meditation and visits with Jesus. After all, on Judgment Day, God will probably not be interested in how much we included in our day, but how much of our day included him.

PRAYER

Almighty Father, the Bible tells us our time is "in your hands." And clearly the key word here is "your," not "my." So when I start obsessing over my schedule, trying to do more than you want me to, help me to slow down. Remind me not to overload myself with commitments and activities that will have me losing sleep, worrying over how I can fit them all in. As for my part, I will make more time for you and focus more on activities that will bring me closer to you. Then, too, with your help, I will keep reminding myself that all the time I really have is the second I am in, that everything important for me to do will get done and that my life is unfolding according to what's in your Day-timer—not mine.

◆　◆　◆

CHAPTER 9

What People Say— What People Think

We are so vain that we even care for the opinion
of those we don't care for.

—MARIE VON EBNER-ESCHENBACH

I am the LORD, the one who encourages you.
Why are you afraid of mere humans?
They dry up and die like grass.

—ISAIAH 51:12 CEV

If God is for us, who can be against us?

—ROMANS 8:31

I care very little if I am judged by you. . . .
It is the Lord who judges me.

—1 CORINTHIANS 4:3, 4

Worry is the warning light that God has been shoved
to the sideline. The moment you put him back at the
center, you will have peace again.

—RICK WARREN

Man goes to heaven, meets Saint Peter at the Pearly Gates. "I see here you're a worrywart," Saint Peter says. "Spent a great deal of time agonizing over what people say and think?" The man shakes his head yes. "Ever worry about what God says or thinks?" Saint Peter asks. The man stutters. "Ah . . . well, sir," he says, "I'm worrying now. Does that count?"

Feeling distressed about what people say and think isn't just something chronic worrywarts do. Everyone's guilty. And can you blame us? Since we were kids we've been inundated with messages that activate anxieties. Statements like "What will the neighbors think?" "What will your father say?" Then, of course, there's the media inviting worry if we don't use a certain toothpaste or cart around the latest laptop.

Put these apprehensions under the microscope, and they do seem pretty silly. After all, people are just people. They come and they go in our lives. Their words and thoughts are just so much puff and stuff. They can't harm us unless we give them the power to do so. Sure, opinions may affect us temporarily, but in the long run, will they matter in a week? A month? A year? Probably not. Then, of course, worrywarts tend to assume the worst. Given that people actually *do* have us on their lips and minds in the first place, we'd fare a lot better imagining it's a benign view.

Truth is, we want to be liked. We want to be accepted. But no one gets high points from everyone. And no amount of worrying will change that. And if we're looking for acceptance, well, why not go to the Source? With God, we just can't lose. He loves us for who we are, warts and all.

Now, isn't it comforting to know someone in high places, someone more powerful and important than anyone on earth, thinks we're special and says he likes us just the way we are? It's enough to make a worrywart stop worrying.

PRAYER

Dear Jesus,

I need your help big-time. This habit is so much a part of me, it's going to be hard to break. Open my eyes so I see that my concerns over what the Joneses think is vain, frivolous and self-defeating; that it puts you second and gives people—even perfect strangers—power to wreck my day. Remind me, when I've gone off track with this energy-sapping behavior, to put the brakes on for a minute and ask myself one question: How many of the people I'm worrying about would die for me as you did? This will help me see how foolish I'm being. It will help me readjust my perspective and remind me there's no one more important than you.

◆ ◆ ◆

CHAPTER 10

Finding a Mate

Delight yourself in the LORD and he will give you the
desires of your heart.

—PSALM 37:4

Matches are made in heaven.

—ROBERT BURTON

God has set the type of marriage everywhere throughout
the creation. Every creature seeks its perfection in another.
The very heavens and earth picture it to us.

—MARTIN LUTHER

There is surely a future hope for you, and your
hope will not be cut off.

—PROVERBS 23:18

For this cause, a man shall leave his father and mother,
and shall cleave to his wife; and the two shall
become one flesh.

—EPHESIANS 5:31 NASB

The art of living is to enjoy what we can see and
not complain about what remains in the dark.

—HENRI J. M. NOUWEN

It is God's will, not merely that we should be happy,
but that we should *make* ourselves happy.

—IMMANUEL KANT

Other than being seen in a bathing suit by anyone at the office,
one of the scariest things a worrywart has to deal with in this
lifetime (and here I'll concentrate on us women, though it's a problem for men as well) is finding a mate. With that in mind, I offer up
a lighthearted fairy tale.

Once upon a time, a woman I know (who looks suspiciously like me) spent years fretting over finding a husband—not so much because she wanted to, but because it was the national female pastime of that century. Back in those antediluvian times, the equation was: woman + marriage = happiness. And with so much at stake, her worrywart juices were constantly overflowing. She worried she wasn't pretty enough or smart enough or helpless enough to find Mr. Right, and that if he didn't come along soon, she'd wind up a tired old maid, living alone on a dusty shelf next to the baked beans and stale crackers.

Needless to say, she prayed often and in earnest that God would put an end to her misery. Yet through it all, she continued to worry, which did nothing for her complexion, not to mention her disposition, which was becoming so caustic, even her close friends avoided her. Then suddenly one day, she had an epiphany. *Was God perhaps trying to tell her something?* she thought. *Did he want her to remain single? Maybe he knew something* (duh) *that she didn't. Maybe she wasn't ready. Or perhaps, maybe he was working something out in her that couldn't happen if she were married. Maybe he wanted her to grow more, experience more. Maybe he wanted her to get to know herself and what she wanted out of life better so she could make a better choice of who she wanted to spend that life with.*

When this finally hit her, she did an about-face. She took off her makeup and high heels, got down on her knees, and right then and there handed the whole search-for-a-mate crusade over to the Almighty. *Dear God,* she prayed, *I'd love to get married, but if being single's the way you want me to live, then so be it.*

Having accepted God's will for her, she was free at last to be the person she was—not the person everyone else wanted her to be. She stopped living her life as a single and started living it as a person. She quit the singles scene and buckled down to her work. Then when all the statistics said she had a better chance of finding oil in a cactus than of finding a mate, she met, fell in love with and married a "nice *young* man." Because she put things in God's hands, he put her precisely where she needed to be when he sent Mr. Right, not on a white horse, but in a burgundy Ford, into her life. And I've, ah . . . she's lived happily ever after since then.

Okay, so the story's about me. But I can't help telling it. It's personal, it's true and I pray it appeals to the sensibilities of worrywarts out there who agonize over finding a mate. I urge you, remember, God knows what you need. And he's more than willing to give it to you.

Now a very wise older man named Evagrius Ponticus explained in a book he wrote called *Chapters on Prayer* that trying to pressure God into giving us what we want, instead of praying for him to help us want the right things—what is *best* for us at the time—is where we run into trouble. Because if what we want isn't in accordance with God's will, things often backfire, he says. Then, too, quite often when we get what we want, it isn't all it was cracked up to be. The smart option, Evagrius wrote, is to "Ask for what is good, and for what is best for your soul. (Because) there is no way you could want these things for yourself more than God desires you to have them."

In the meantime, though, do me a favor. Please. Get rid of the notion that because you haven't met your soul mate as yet, life is something to be tolerated until he comes along. Instead, live the life God has put in front of you today. Don't make yourself crazy with worry over something that might not happen today, but, if it's God's will, could certainly happen tomorrow or next week or next month. Because when Mr. Wonderful does come along, you don't want to have so many worry lines that you scare him off, now, do you?

P.S. This business of letting go really works. If you don't believe my story, consider the apostles. They fished all night until they were dog-tired, but they didn't catch a thing. Yet as soon as they gave up, Jesus was able to fill their nets to breaking. You can tell God you aren't interested in lots of fish in the sea . . . you're just looking for the right one.

PRAYER

Dearest Father,

I know you're the best matchmaker around, so I've got to believe you will find me a perfect mate. But I can't expect you to answer my prayers when I'm acting like I don't believe you will. So I'm placing my husband-hunting in your hands. And from now on, I'm going to stop obsessing and enjoy my single life instead of living each day as though it were a bus terminal, a stopover until my happiness ride comes along. Help me to remember that, whether married or single, I'm responsible for my own sense of well-being. And with your help, I will regain it and keep it. Oh, and, God, please make him like cats! (Feel free to insert your choice of pet here.)

◆　◆　◆

CHAPTER 11

Job Jitters

Men, for the sake of getting a living, forget to live.

—MARGARET FULLER

"For I know the plans I have for you," declares the LORD,
"plans to prosper you and not to harm you, plans to
give you hope and a future."

—JEREMIAH 29:11

God never shuts one door but he opens another.

—IRISH PROVERB

Mary Alpert was reorganized out of her job. She joined another company and was doing fine until that company merged with the company that originally reengineered her and—you guessed it—Mary was laid off again.

Nowadays, through no fault of our own, we find ourselves stuck under a cloud of pink slips and unemployment lines. Worriers who have a job fret over losing it. Those who've lost theirs wring their hands over finding something new. For people like us, even the hint of downsizing puts us in a tailspin. We're on edge, unable to concentrate, certain the worst is headed our way. When passing the boss's closed door, we shiver. The boss looks our way, we shake. We try putting negative thoughts out of our heads, but can't seem to. Everywhere we go, visions of Ms. Human Resources handing us a layoff packet, with a sweet smile and a hearty "Have a nice life," haunt us.

Still, in this economic climate, it would be foolish *not* to worry. We have obligations. The bank could foreclose. The dentist could reclaim the kids' fillings. The cat could threaten to leave.

And the sky could fall in our soup. Ridiculous? Not for worrywarts. Hey, this is what we do best. We throw out a million different scenarios, when God's already written the play. And we're not giving him even the slightest bit of credit. We've forgotten he didn't just make us, then say, "I'm out of here. Fend for yourself." He gave his word to always be with us, work for our good and give us all we need. Worrying sells him short.

How do we quit? Living in the present is a good way to start. It's advice we've heard a billion times. Jesus himself says, "Do not worry about tomorrow, for tomorrow will worry about itself." Goethe reminds us that "all really intelligent men recognize that the moment is everything," and Fra Giovanni tells us, "No heaven can come to us unless our hearts find rest in today. Take heaven!" By living in the here and now, minute by minute, we can take control and make the most of our days. Try it. Then when tomorrow comes, we can enjoy that, too. Little by little, we'll learn to stop letting fear of what *might* happen rob of us of the joy of what *is* happening. Bottom line is, whatever the outcome, we'll have lived each day to the hilt in the meantime.

PRAYER

Lord, please give me the grace to put aside my worries over work. Let me live in the moment and be grateful for the job I have right now. Keep me from ruining my day with paranoia about whether I'll have my job tomorrow. I know you know what's best for me. So help me remember you will always give me what I need (which may not always correspond with what I want). And if your plans do include a pink slip, help me flex my faith muscle and trust the new road you're putting me on. Teach me to understand that what I consider a setback is actually your way of moving me forward in a positive direction. Finally, help me look at any work-related challenge you put before me as an opportunity to grow, secure in the knowledge you want me to succeed and find joy.

◆　◆　◆

CHAPTER 12

Fueling Anxiety with Negativity

Two men look out through the same bars:
One sees the mud, and one the stars.

—FREDERICK LANGBRIDGE

Test everything. Hold on to the good.
Avoid every kind of evil.

—1 THESSALONIANS 5:21, 22

When anxiety was great within me, your
consolation brought joy to my soul.

—PSALM 94:19

The "peace of God" is the opposite of anxiety.
It is tranquillity that comes when believers commit all
their cares to God in prayer and worry about them no more.

—NOTE ON PHILIPPIANS 4:7 IN THE NIV

If we give negative thinking an inch, it will take four thousand yards. That's just the way a worrywart's mind works. So to stop our anxieties from escalating, all we have to do is eliminate negativity from our minds.

In never-never land, that might be possible. But in reality, it's a tall order. Especially since when we get into a problem and start to feel anxious, we exacerbate the situation. So when one bad thing happens, instead of trying to figure out a positive solution, we stay stuck on the downside. This ignites negative energy and causes another real or imaginary bad thing to happen, then another and another. It's as if by giving in to negativity, we inadvertently play a role in setting ourselves up for more trouble. Then we stand back and say, "Aha. I knew it. There . . . you see," in confirmation.

This tends to happen when we're having "one of those days." These are the times we feel out of synch with God and the universe. Nothing is going right. We can't win for losing. Or, like Job, we feel maybe God is testing our faith, our problem-solving techniques or both. I remember the night it happened to me. My car died near a dangerous off-ramp. (*Transmission or engine trouble for sure.*) It was dark and foggy. I had my cell phone, but the battery was low.

(*Figures.*) So I put on my flashers, got out of the car and tried to flag someone down. (*No one is stopping!*) I looked for a way to the street. But (*Oh, no!*) the highway was fenced in. So I kept walking until I found a place to squeeze through and (*Here we go again!*) tore my coat. I finally found a phone, but my house number was busy. (*When is this nightmare going to end?*) So by the time I reached my husband, I had worked myself into such a frenzy that I cried into the phone, "Help me. My car is smashed," and hung up, without ever telling him where I was. The poor man had to drive up and down the highway until he found me standing by my car with a tow truck man and a state trooper.

Now this scenario could have played out much differently if I hadn't let negativity get the upper hand. I could have said to myself, *Yes, I'm stuck on the side of the road. Yes, it is foggy and dark. But I'm not going to get mired in a knee-jerk, emotional panic. I'm going to ask God to help me think clearly and figure out a solution.* With calming thoughts of a loving, protective God, and a more positive attitude, I'd have been much better able to roll with the punches— maybe even laugh at the fiasco while it was happening, as I do now when I tell the story.

It's not the bad things that happen to us that make us nuts; it's our reactions to them—what the little voices in our heads, aka our thoughts, tell us about the situation. And here we have a choice. We can, with God's help and some self-determination, be superheroes who zap negativity, solve the problem and save the day. Or we can be negativity victims, who spiral out of control, make matters worse and prove to ourselves just how bad life is. (*See, I told you it's awful.*) My vote's for the superheroes. But to be one, we need to have an action plan that enlists God's help the minute something bad happens. I now have one I'd like to share. First, I say this get-me-back-on-track prayer I found in the Psalms: "Hasten, O God, to save me; O LORD, come quickly to help me," followed by my own petition: "God, I want to work this out with a clear mind, and I need your help to keep my emotions under control while I do." Then I look for three things that are *right* with the situation, and proceed from there.

The time I spend praying calms me, gives me strength and helps me get my bearings. Looking for the positive readjusts my outlook and puts me in a better position to ask, "What can I do about this?" instead of complaining, "This is the most awful thing that's happened to me, and I just know there's more ahead."

As for my car, negativity really played me to the hilt. What happened? Nothing catastrophic and hardly cause for hysteria. I had done something I had never done in my life: run out of gas. (*Wouldn't you know?*)

PRAYER

Dearest God,

Starting today, Lord, with your help, I will not let negativity drag me under like quicksand. I'm well aware from past episodes how insidious it is. So I'm going to be more vigilant. From now on, I'm going to acknowledge what my difficulties are, assess them from a positive perspective first, then, with your strength and guidance, use the brain you gave me in a calm manner to figure out some viable solutions. I know this is easier said than done, Lord, so if I start to freak out, I pray, as the psalmist did, for you to "Hasten, O God, and save me; O Lord, come quickly to help me."

◆ ◆ ◆

Neat to a Fault

Martha rushed around the house,
Too busy for the Lord.
But Mary sat at Jesus' feet,
And listened to His Word.

Oh to be like Mary,
and near to Jesus stay,
To listen to His precious Word,
And talk to Him each day.

—MARILYN LASHBROOK

Dust protects the furniture.

—ANONYMOUS

Set your minds on things above, not on earthly things.

—COLOSSIANS 3:2

As for me and my household, we will serve the LORD.

—JOSHUA 24:15

E xcessive fussiness and worrying go together like a dustpan and brush. And there's no better example than the story of Martha, the Bible's Worrywart poster girl, and Mary, her much-maligned-for-not-helping sister.

Here's the scene. Martha's in the kitchen preparing the meal. Mary's in the living room making her guest feel at home. Everything's copacetic until Martha's inner musings start setting her up for disaster. It begins with a simple thought. *Everything's got to be just right for this dinner,* she says to herself. *After all, Jesus isn't just company; he's our friend and Savior.* Then in creep some doubts. *I should have started earlier. He must be starving.* Doubts turn thoughts into false reality. *Jesus is starving and I don't have a thing ready for him.* And in marches anxiety. *I'm late with the meal. What am I going to do? He must really think I'm an awful hostess.*

Martha's on a roll. Her thoughts get more chaotic as they churn—until anxiety gives way to another emotion: anger. She looks for a scapegoat, and poor Mary's sitting in the line of fire. *Look at her,* Martha fumes. *I'm out here slaving away for our guest and what's my precious sister doing? Nothing! She should be in here helping me. I'd like to listen to Jesus, too. But somebody's got to do the work.* So the anger escalates, and pretty soon Martha's embroiling Jesus in the fracas.

Now Jesus knew Martha's anxieties didn't all stem from wanting to please him—that part of them came from her own insecurities. Yes, she wanted things to be perfect. But not so much because it would make *Jesus* feel better if they were, but because *she'd* feel better. And it was the fear that she was falling short of the mark that put her in a panic. Another guess is she was feeling kind of left out and put upon.

So when she said, "Lord, don't you care that my sister has left *me* to do all the work by *myself?* Tell her to help me!" What she was really saying is, "Jesus, you're not paying attention to me. And you are not appreciating me . . . and this, after all I'm doing for you."

Now, someone not as gentle as Jesus might have said, "No, Martha, you've got this thing backward. You're not paying attention to me. You are not appreciating me . . . and this, after all *I'm* doing for *you.*" Indeed, someone not as kind as Jesus might have said, "Martha, stop your fussing. I don't care if we eat locusts and well water. Settle down. I came for the company, not the food." But all Jesus said was, "Martha, Martha. You are worried and upset about many things, but only one thing is needed. Mary has chosen what is better, and it will not be taken away from her."

See, Jesus knows we worrywarts are a struggling bunch. And he knew in this instance Martha meant well. The problem was, though, she was more involved with the process than with the person. Her mind was "distracted" with everything *but* her guest. God's in the details, they say. But in this case, he was in the living room, waiting for her to make him feel welcome. Mary, on the other hand, sat enrapt, totally oblivious to anything but Jesus. He was explaining the most wonderful things to her about God and heaven, so she literally dropped everything and gave all her attention to him. What's more, she might have even guessed her sister would throw a tantrum. But she didn't care. Whatever transpired, Mary wasn't worried. She was focused.

Now, since "distracted" is a worrywart's middle name, we can learn a lot from this story. At the top of the list is why it's important to get our priorities straight. So if we feel we'll wind up like Martha—harried and angry—we'd be better off making the choice that Mary did—namely, to drop everything and take a Jesus break. And while we're at it, we can ask him to keep our worrywart minds from being mired in things nobody really cares about. Because if we can remember to "seek first his kingdom and his righteousness," we can rest assured everything else will turn out okay—including the dinner.

PRAYER

Dearest Jesus,

Like Martha, I am often fussing over trivialities and not giving you the time and attention you deserve. But with your help, I can put that behind me. From now on, I won't only come to you with a complaint, a request or a problem. I'll come for some quiet time alone, for no special reason, other than to sit at your feet . . . no hassle, no fuss . . . and just visit.

◆ ◆ ◆

CHAPTER 14

Who Stole My Body?

Charm is deceptive and beauty is fleeting, but a
woman who fears the LORD is to be praised.

—PROVERBS 31:30

I consider everything a loss compared to the surpassing
greatness of knowing Christ Jesus my Lord, for whose sake
I have lost all things. I consider them rubbish. . . .

—PHILIPPIANS 3:8

Everybody's youth is a dream, a form of chemical madness.

—F. SCOTT FITZGERALD

Flee the evil desires of youth and pursue righteousness.

—2 TIMOTHY 2:22

. . . who satisfies your desires with good things, so
that your youth is renewed like the eagle's.

—PSALM 103:5

As we become older, we become like old cars—
more and more repairs and replacements are necessary.
We must just look forward to the fine new machines
(latest Resurrection model) which are waiting for us,
we hope, in the Divine garage!

—C. S. LEWIS

*H*air graying? Chin sagging? Wrinkles around the eyes? Face it,
for most people, losing our looks is no ride in the park. But for
worrywarts, it's as though our one and only friend is leaving for the
coast, and we're trying every trick in the book to make her stay.

Oh my goodness, we fret, our foreheads look like tire treads. And
oh my gosh, we moan, our skin is drier than an empty canteen.
We're sagging here and puffing out there. We're jiggling here and
drooping down there. Our heads are balding while our upper lips
grow enough hair for a small wig. And those mirrors that used to be

friends? Well, they've turned on us. And no matter how many times we check ourselves out at the bathroom sink or in the reflections of store windows, it's always the same: we don't recognize the person we see. It's enough to make us call 911. "A stranger's invaded my body," we'll report. "And I don't know what she's done with me."

Okay, so we've lost youth's first blush (and then some). But having a panic attack over our looks can only make matters worse. Everyone knows stress is a killer, and anxiety can make us older before our time. Some people even say it causes tooth decay. So worry can only add to our problems. What we need is a change of attitude. The psalmist wasn't kidding when he said, "Because of the sound of my groaning, my bones cling to my skin." Better to be calm and happy, he urges, since "a tranquil heart is life to the body," and "a joyful heart makes a cheerful face."

It's not as if we can do a lot to change things. Oh, sure, we could try skin peels, botox and sheep cell replacement. But that's just a stopgap. Besides, those kinds of treatments are worrisome in themselves. Who knows where they could lead? Like a lot of people who try to keep the bloom on the rose, we run the risk of becoming addicted to the good results. So, for example, if we had collagen once, we may do it again. And if we had surgery twice, we may do it a third, maybe even a fourth, time. By then, like a rubber band around a piano, our skin would be pulled so taut, we could blow our heads off when we sneezed. And that would *really* be something to worry about. No matter what we do, inevitably, earthly beauty fades. And fretting about trying to stop it is about as futile as trying to stop a bud turning into a leaf, or a day turning into night.

We'd be better off focusing on what we think the purpose of this stage of our lives is all about. A good guess is God's trying to give us a wake-up call. He's trying to remind us that the things of the flesh are transient, and if we haven't already, we'd better start getting our spiritual affairs in order. In my opinion, God throws baldness, droopy eyes and middle age our way as signposts. It's his way of reminding us we ought to stop being superficial and self-absorbed and start being more introspective and spiritually mature. We should not "speak like a child, think like a child, reason like a child," but rather, "put childish ways behind us."

After all, our purpose here is not to win eternal beauty, but eternal life. And what comes with that, the Bible tells us, is Jesus's promise to "transform our lowly bodies, so that they will be like his glorious body." Surely a promise like that should be enough to keep us worrywarts from obsessing. Think about it: a few wrinkles in the here and now, then, if we have faith in Christ and do his will, a glorious body in the hereafter. If that doesn't ease our furrowed brows, nothing will. Remember, Jesus said, "Whoever loses his life for my sake will find it." So the next time we see a gray hair, let's say, "Thank you, Jesus." And the next time he hands us age spots, let's play connect the dots.

PRAYER

Dear Lord,

I'm such a vain thing—always looking in the mirror. You'd think I thought I was going to disappear. Truth is, my old body will do just that, but you promised to give me a brand-new one. Yet, my body's not the thing you're interested in. It's my soul. So help me concentrate all my efforts on making it as desirable as possible. Let me put on the creams of forgiveness to make it soft and subtle, the makeup of love to cover my rough spots and a radiant garment of faith to make me beautiful in your sight.

◆ ◆ ◆

CHAPTER 15

Accepting Joy

Joy is the echo of God's life within us.

—JOSEPH MARMION

It was joy and peace, which Jesus said
he left men in his will.

—KIRBY PAGE

If you have no joy . . . there's a leak in your
Christianity somewhere.

—A. SUNDAY

Be joyful always; pray continually.

—1 THESSALONIANS 5:16

I delight greatly in the LORD.

—ISAIAH 61:10

The thief comes only in order to steal, kill, and destroy. I came that they may have and enjoy life, and have it in abundance.

—JOHN 10:10

Be joyful always.

—1 THESSALONIANS 5:16

Our lives are what our thoughts make them.

—MARCUS AURELIUS

It's a sorry state of affairs, and a sad reality, but worrywarts find it hard to accept joy. We feel uncomfortable with it, as though someone had given us a gift we don't deserve. We feel suspicious of it, asking ourselves, "Why am I so happy when lots of others aren't?" And we feel a sense of dread because of it, an I-can't-quite-put-my-finger-on-why feeling that something bad is waiting in the wings—and the proverbial other shoe is about to drop.

What a bummer—especially since that is so *not* what God wants for us. We need only open the Bible for confirmation. I did, and counted 246-plus entries under the heading "joy," a sampling of which shows God filling people with joy, wanting our "joy to be complete," ending grief with joy, promising no one will take away our joy, telling us to be joyful always, plus dozens of entries where people were shouting to God for joy, drank wine with joy, danced for joy, and had hearts that were swelling, throbbing and literally bursting out of their togas with joy.

What's more, the Bible tells us that Jesus "came so that [we] may have and enjoy life, and have it in abundance," and that God, like a doting parent, wants to fill our lives "with good things." Jesus stresses the point further, explaining that even evil people give their kids good gifts. And if that's the case, how much more [joy] can we expect from our Heavenly Parent? And the disciple, Paul, tells us we can't even *imagine* what God has in store for us now and in the future, explaining that "no eye has seen, no ear has heard, no mind has conceived what [joy] God has prepared for those who love him." Boy, you'd think worrywarts would get it.

Okay, so if we take it as a given that God delights in our joy, why can't we? Why, when we should be knee-deep in happiness, are we spoiling our joy by anticipating bad things? Who's playing tricks with our minds? Was it something we picked up in our childhood—a warning, "Don't be too happy or something awful will happen"? Or maybe we listened too often to negative people—the devil's joy zappers—who've blocked God out, and as a result can never be happy and don't want anyone else to be. Whatever the reason, we have to align ourselves more closely with God, so we can stop looking over our shoulders and get these anxiety demons to take a hike.

"The world will make you suffer," Jesus said, but he also said, "Be brave. I have defeated the world." But suffering and trouble don't come because we're too happy. God doesn't serve a dinner of happiness and a dessert of misery. On the contrary, he gives us joy without strings. All we have to do is invite him into our lives, because there can be no joy without him, period. But with him, everything—not just big-ticket items like finding the perfect mate and an awesome job—but everyday experiences like discovering a parking space close to the shops or a cat with milk on his face—becomes a joyous reflection of his love.

So never be weary of joy. Look for it in everything and accept it graciously and with thanksgiving, as a benevolent gift from a loving Father. And, remember, there's plenty more where it came from.

PRAYER

Dear Lord,

You know I'm a work in progress. And you know that, despite everything you've said and everything you do for me, I have this chronic worrywart problem: I feel nervous when I'm happy. I know you didn't send Jesus to die for me so that I could wallow in dread. So please help me get it into my head that by getting closer to you, I can experience joy every day, under any circumstance, because your love banishes fear. Help me get rid of my gloomy thoughts as well as guard against others who want to zap my joy. Fill me with the happiness, peace and calm that come from knowing you in this life, and from anticipating being with you in the life to come.

◆ ◆ ◆

CHAPTER 16

Now I rejoice, not that you were made sorry,
but that your sorrow led to repentance.

—2 CORINTHIANS 7:9 NKJV

And God shall wipe away all tears from their eyes;
and there shall be no more death, neither sorrow,
nor crying, neither shall there be any more pain:
for the former things are passed away.

—REVELATION 21:4 KJV

For we have not an high priest which cannot be
touched with the feeling of our infirmities . . .

—HEBREWS 4:15 KJV

But I would not have you to be ignorant, brethren,
concerning them which are asleep, that ye sorrow not,
even as others which have no hope. For if we believe that
Jesus died and rose again, even so them also which
sleep in Jesus will God bring with him.

—1 THESSALONIANS 4:13–15 KJV

Those who live in the Lord never see
each other for the last time.

—GERMAN PROVERB

I am the resurrection and the life. He who believes
in me will live, even though he dies; and whoever lives
and believes in me will never die.

—JOHN 11:25, 26

When it comes to anxiety about loss, I'm no expert. I can only offer my own story and hope it helps the worrywart in you believe God can bring something good out of something awful, even grief.

My father and I were like conjoined twins—we were that close. I could never remember a time his light didn't shine on me. He had an abundant sense of humor and could talk to a busy signal. So much so, his friends at the senior center made up some "business cards" for him one day. On them, they listed his specialty as "free, unsolicited advice." He was always on the go, even if it was just walking up and down the driveway after a hip operation. His spirit was a mustang that could not be bridled.

He was sick for what seemed an eternity—but was mercifully about two years. So I taxied him to doctors and specialists near and far. He had a weird swallowing problem that made him aspirate— we know it as food going down the wrong pipe. Though things were quite grave, we never took them seriously. We somehow always made these jaunts humorous. We kept up the facade really well. But ultimately, my father stopped eating and slowly withered away. I watched him and I worried—that he would die, and that he wouldn't.

When he finally succumbed, anxiety took me over completely. I worried that I couldn't go on, that the pain would never stop, that I'd lose my mind, that I'd never be able to function again. I worried that I'd alienate my friends and the man I loved, my husband of ten months. I worried that nothing would ever have meaning for me again, that I could never hold a job, write, sleep, taste joy or pleasure. I worried I would never ever shake the panic, and the indescribably heavyhearted feeling of numbness and despair that enveloped me.

I walked around in a somnambulistic fog. I prayed, but I was just going through the motions. Nothing could penetrate my sorrow. I felt sick to my stomach from morning to night. I could get no relief. Then when I thought I would literally dissolve from grief, I crept into an empty, dark church, sat down and, sobbing uncontrollably, told God I couldn't go on. I told him I would not make it a second longer and would die right then and there of a heartbreak overdose if he didn't grant me mercy and help me out. I said I was sorry for waiting until the worst had happened to get serious about my relationship with him. I begged him to forgive me and give me strength.

Suffice it to say, the skies didn't open up, and the Lord didn't say, "There, there, you're forgiven. Everything will be fine from now on." However, I do think what happened was that, unbeknownst to me, when I was totally emptied out, devoid of every drop of my being, Jesus stepped in. He came quietly without fanfare. Though I didn't realize it at the time, he put his arms around me, comforted me, accepted my apology and gave me the strength to live another day, because for the first time since my father died, I felt I could.

Still, this was no overnight healing. The heartsickness I experienced was by no means taken away. In fact, it intensified, because now I was grieving doubly, over the loss of my father and the loss of years spent apathetic to God. Yet God knew this had to happen. So he let me experience it all. And there was only one reason I was now able to bear it: Jesus helped me.

He sat near me in the kitchen while I listened to Wagner, day after day, cried my eyes out and painted the cupboard, over and over again. He kept me company at countless lunches where I pushed my food around the plate, then finally threw it out. He went on dozens of wild goose chases with me as I walked up and down the stairs of my house, forgetting what I was doing or where I was going. He rocked me to sleep at night in the spare room where I went to muffle my tears so my husband could get a little sleep. And he let me take my time and grieve my own way. He never once tried to speed things up so my pain would lessen or I'd learn to live with it quicker.

He just followed me around, in the shadows, everywhere I went, helping me carry my cross. He supported me as I went through this most difficult experience. That was ten years ago, and, though I never got over the loss, I did get on with my life.

So, despite all my anxieties, Jesus turned my apocalypse into my saving grace. He used my pain to bring me back to him—not just for the time being, but for always. I talk to him everyday now—not just when I need something or am in a jam—and, though I do strike out a lot because of sin, at least now I'm in the ballpark. Experts say people who've been through life's tough times are really the best types to get others through their pain. Jesus is that person. He's experienced it all. The Bible says, "In all their distress, [the LORD] too was distressed." I believe it. He feels our pain because he felt the same pain himself.

Truth is, we're none of us getting out of this life without experiencing loss. So the worry is not that it happens, because it will. The worry is, how will we deal with it?

The Bible says, "Come boldly to the throne of our gracious God. There . . . we will find grace to help us when we need it," and "Cast your burden on the Lord, and he will sustain you." I did—unfortunately not out of faith, but out of desperation. It didn't matter to him. He helped me out anyway. I know if you ask, he will do the same for you, too.

PRAYER

Dearest Jesus,

When I write about the mess I was in when my father died, I feel my heart pierced all over again—but it's not the cannon that went through it the first time. It's a dull ache that will probably never go away. Looking back, I know I could not have gotten through this horrendous time without you. So I thank you, Lord, for being there. I also thank you for not letting my pain go to waste. Thanks for using it to bring me back to you. I hope people reading this won't wait as long as I did to firm up their relationship with you, because a life without God is really a loss. P.S. Lord, say hi to my Pop-o for me, will you?

◆ ◆ ◆

CHAPTER 17

Change—The Worrywart's Friend

It is only the wisest and the very stupidest
that cannot change.

—CONFUCIUS

Do not conform any longer to the pattern of this world,
but be transformed by the renewing of your mind.

—ROMANS 12:2

There is nothing permanent, except change.

—HERACLITUS

Is any man afraid of change? Why, what can take place
without change? What then is more pleasing or more
suitable to the universal nature?

—MARCUS AURELIUS

I, the LORD, do not change.

—MALACHI 3:6

For the trumpet will sound, the dead will be
raised imperishable, and we will be changed.

—1 CORINTHIANS 15:52

Most people would rather stick a scorpion up their noses than
embrace change. Hyperbole? Perhaps. But for many, change
is synonymous with upheaval, loss, fear, disappointment and failure.
Sameness, like an old slipper, feels more comfortable. So people
would just as soon live with the status quo. It's not perfect, they reason. But it's what they're used to. Past experience has taught them:
change is nobody's friend. So who needs it?

Worrywarts do. For us it's the best thing since low-carb pasta.
Change offers hope, renewal and a window of opportunity. It helps
us surrender our anxieties to God, practice faith and trust, and
reprogram our thoughts away from confusion and fear, toward clarity

and joyfulness. We have nothing to lose (but our worries), and everything to gain (our sanity). So what's not to like about change?

Still, we wouldn't be worrywarts if we didn't ask: what if we try to change and can't? Well, God knows, we can't transform on our own. But through the power of the Holy Spirit, change is very doable. The Bible says, "the Spirit of the LORD will come upon you in power . . . and you will be changed into a different person," and "If any man is in Christ, he is a new creature; the old things passed away; behold, new things have come."

But we can't just talk the talk. We have to walk the walk. After we ask God to help us change, we have to *surrender* to his timetable, and be willing to *do the work* that will make change happen, and do it with patience and perseverance. It's not enough to just say, "Okay, I want to change. I want to stop worrying." We need to place our petitions before the Lord; then we must follow our good intentions with positive actions.

Keeping busy is a good place to start. It forces us to refocus our thoughts, even if it's just for a little while. Pray, read Scripture, call a friend, watch a movie, skip rope, write a book, put on an exercise video, paint a picture, sew a quilt, make lasagna, learn Portuguese—anything that requires concentration will do the trick. Even better, if we can do something selfless for someone—volunteer at a hospital or a food bank, visit a sick friend, offer to mind a neighbor's toddler while she goes shopping—we'll be thinking of ourselves less, which is a great way to stave off worry.

Don't go bananas, though, if the heebie-jeebies return. It took us a long time to get to this harried state. So we can't expect a total 360 overnight. The Bible tells us to "put off your old self, which is being corrupted . . . and put on the new self, created to be like God." But it also says, "You too must be patient. . . ."

Look at the disciples. They had Jesus in the flesh to remind them not to be anxious, not to be afraid. Yet even they continued to be anxious when it came time for him to feed a crowd of five thousand, save them from a storm or find money to pay the tax collector. So we can see how guileful worrywarting can be. Still, a good start is half the work. And even if we manage to hold our angst at bay for one half hour a day, or maybe ten times a week, we're headed in the right direction. Because any time we spend free of self-inflicted, unnecessary anxiety shows us we can change and we are changing.

PRAYER

Dearest God,

I need your help if I'm ever going to change. So please hear me, Lord, and change me. Alone, I'm such a weakling. But with your help, I know things can be better. Transform me, Lord, so I don't wind up so comfortable with worry that I'm too complacent to change. I want to break this debilitating habit, and I'm ready to start today. I know I will have to do some serious work to change—and I'm ready to face it. I also know I'm not going to do it all in one day. So give me patience, Lord. And help me persevere. And if I fail, Lord, I won't worry. I know you'll pick me up and we can start again. I know I can be stronger every day if I lean on you. See, Lord, I'm changing already.

◆ ◆ ◆

CHAPTER 18

Don't Worry, Be Silly

Healthy laughter is a shared experience of a moment
of joy. . . . It can also reflect a needed recognition of our
own shortcomings and foolishness. . . .

—DANIEL TAYLOR

Fill today with fun and senseless silliness.

—ANONYMOUS

There is a paradox in pride: it makes some men ridiculous,
but prevents others from becoming so.

—CHARLES CALEB COLTON

But they kept quiet because on the way they had argued about who was the greatest. Sitting down, Jesus called the twelve and said, "If anyone wants to be first, he must be the very last, and the servant of all."

—MARK 9:33–35

The first step (in acquiring humility) is to realize that one is proud. And a biggish step, too. At least, nothing whatever can be done before it. If you think you are not conceited, it means you are very conceited indeed.

—C. S. LEWIS

There's not a lot written about Jesus's sense of humor. But I'd venture to guess if he were around today, he might give his blessing to what I'm about to propose: a national Don't Worry, Be Silly Day. This would be a day we'd set aside to stop everything we're doing and take a hard look at all the things that make us so anxious. Once a year, then, we'd get to see how silly it is to place such importance on things like wealth, looks, status, prestige and power. And once a year, we'd get to see how silly we are when we take ourselves so seriously.

Dress on this day would be simple: no Tommy Hilfiger or designer sweats, just really plain, old, baggy clothes and flip-flops.

Hats would be encouraged—and of course, the sillier, the better. Women would not wear makeup and men would not have to shave. So no one would have to worry about what to wear or how they looked because everyone would look the same—silly.

All cell phones and laptops would be banned, and everyone would have to leave his BMW or Lexus at home and use either stilts or a pogo stick to get places. What's more, no one would reveal who they really were and what they really did. Instead, if anyone asked, each person would pretend he worked at some job the very opposite of his own. This way, one day a year, we would all see how it feels to walk in our neighbors' shoes.

Meals on this day would be simple, too. Every town would have a huge fair, offering tables of smiley-faced peanut butter and jelly sandwiches, chocolate milk served with twirly straws and dessert cups of fake eyeballs in red Jell-O. No low-carb, low-fat food or arugula would be allowed. Caffe lattes, cranberry seltzer and designer springwater would be nixed as well. The good news is no one would go hungry on this day because the food would be free. The bad news is anyone mentioning a diet would have to eat two banana splits with sprinkles.

Singing and dancing would be encouraged—regardless of ability. And if a worrywart always wanted to play the oboe but felt embarrassed, this would be the day to do it. There would be Silly Putty sculpture exhibitions and open mike sessions with topics like "The Silly Things I Worry About." Competitive or status sports would be a no-no. But anyone who had always wanted to bungee jump, climb a wall, go skateboarding or ride a unicycle, but never had an opportunity, could give it a whirl. This way, since no one would take anything seriously, we could try things we have always wanted to do and not have to worry about doing poorly. Happily, we would all get the chance, as Jesus encouraged us, to "become as little children" again.

Best of all, since the mood would be carefree and silly, there would be no one to hate and nothing to fight about. And anyone caught sporting a furrowed brow would get a pie in his face, either chocolate fudge or banana cream.

Now, just before the close of Don't Worry, Be Silly Day, there would be a contest. The object would be to explain how being silly one entire day could help us stop being anxious for the other 364. Since no one's answer would be any better than anyone else's, everyone would be a winner. And the prize would be learning how to worry less and laugh at ourselves more.

PRAYER

Dearest Jesus,

Of all the people you've made, I'm probably the silliest. That's because I'm full of pride and ridiculous notions of self-importance. These faults constantly have me worrying over the most inane things, when what I really should be doing is praising you for your goodness and thanking you for being so tolerant of my big ego. I know a gold card won't get me into heaven, and a title won't get me a better room in your Father's house. So help me to stop being anxious about such nonsense. Help me remember what you told the apostles—that if I want to be first in your eyes, I should practice being last. And if I want to make a good impression on you, I had better start serving instead of demanding to be served. Finally, Lord, help me remember that I am special, but not because of what I have or how important (I think) I am, but because you love me.

◆ ◆ ◆

CHAPTER 19

Possessive Possessions

Dogs do not ruin their sleep worrying about how to keep the objects they have and to obtain the objects they have not.

—EUGENE O'NEILL

Your spirit is exposed to as many hazards as the things you love.

—GUIGO I

Set your mind on the things above, not on the things that are on earth.

—COLOSSIANS 3:2 NASB

A man's life does not consist in the
abundance of his possessions.

—LUKE 12:15

Provide purses for yourself that will not wear out,
a treasure in heaven that will not be exhausted, where
no thief comes near and no moth destroys. For where
your treasure is, there your heart will be also.

—LUKE 12:32–34

Uprooting of worry is losing your attachments to things.

—BUDDHA

And how does a man benefit if he gains the whole
world and loses his soul in the process?

—MARK 8:36 TLB

Let the moment come when nothing is left but life,
and you will find that you do not hesitate over
the fate of material possessions.

—EDDIE RICKENBACKER

A friend of mine told me this story: An old woman she knew asked her daughter if she could arrange for a Dumpster.

"What in the world do you want with that?" the woman's daughter asked.

"I want to get rid of my worries," she said, then continued. "My rings and my furniture, my silverware, even the dog. I'm getting rid of everything. See, I've finally figured it out," the woman said with conviction. "If I don't have anything, I won't have anything to worry about."

The daughter looked at her mom as though she had three heads.

"But, Mom," she protested, "these are antiques. Don't throw them away. I'll take them."

The old woman leaned in and cupped her daughter's face lovingly.

"Honey," she said, "you're not listening. I want to get rid of my worries, not pass them on."

Like the old lady in the story, worrywarts would be a lot better off if we could loosen the grip our possessions have on us, because 99 percent of our anxieties come as a result of our fixations on "stuff." First, we fuss and fret over whether we'll be able to get whatever it is. (Half the time, we don't even know if we *really* want it.) Once we get it, we worry ourselves sick because we're afraid we'll lose it. Meantime, we've totally lost sight of the fact that God gives us things to use—not hold us captive. We eat off a plate. We don't obsess over it. We just use it. If we lose it, we won't be heartbroken. If it breaks, we'll get another. We don't think to ourselves, *Well, if I don't have this plate, I can't eat dinner.* We figure something out. We don't give the plate so much power that it affects our lives. Yet that's exactly what we do when we worry over things like our car, our furniture, our diamond rings.

We should know better, because Jesus's message couldn't be clearer: It's not about the stuff, people. If he said it once, he said it a dozen times. Don't worry about things—food, drink or clothes. To hammer the point in further, he gave examples of the foolish man who spent his life storing up grain and riches, then died before he could enjoy them, and the rich man who might have been sitting with Jesus in heaven this very minute, but for his love of "stuff" that has long since disintegrated.

So there are two ways we can go. We can either stay obsessively preoccupied with material goods, worry over them, fuss over them, make them our lives and threaten our chance for eternal life. Or we can fixate ourselves on Jesus, temper our longings for belongings and, as a result, do away with the worry and turmoil we experience because of them. The only thing we can't do, Jesus says, is "serve two masters."

The flip side of this is that Jesus knows we have wants and needs—we were created with them. And he's not advocating we all become ascetics. He's not telling us to withdraw from the enjoyment material goods bring. Indeed, the same Jesus who told us not to concern ourselves with earthly possessions also told us that if we want something, "Ask, and it will be given." So he's more than willing to give us things to use and enjoy. He's just warning us not to get so caught up in them that we forget about him, others and what we're supposed to be doing here on earth in the first place. And contrary to what a bumper sticker I saw on a Hummer read, it's not "The guy who dies with the most toys wins."

Still, maybe we're not ready—like the woman in the story—to throw *all* our possessions out to avoid worrying about them. But perhaps we can start detaching a little at a time until we can get to the point where we look at things as just that: things. If we have them, fine. If we don't, that's fine, too. Then they won't control our lives and be the source of so much Sturm und Drang. Maybe then we can say with Paul, "I know what it is to be in need, and I know what it is to have plenty. I have learned the secret of being content in any and every situation, whether well fed or hungry, whether living in plenty or in want." Now that would really be worth something.

PRAYER

Dearest God,

I have too much stuff. It makes me fret and worry and waste time I should be using more productively. So, starting today, I'm going to make an effort to wean myself off "things." Teach me, Lord, to value, use and enjoy the material gifts you give me, but not make them my be-all and end-all. Help me to give away more and buy less so I can experience the peace that comes from detaching myself from meaningless objects. Lord, help me learn the lesson Paul did, so I can be satisfied in any circumstance, safe in the knowledge that you're always taking care of me. And finally, Lord, help me remember that the treasure I'd be better off worrying about is the one I won't find in any store.

◆ ◆ ◆

CHAPTER 20

Timing

All that I have seen teaches me to trust the
Creator for all I have not seen.

—RALPH WALDO EMERSON

There is no guarantee that if we had done a part of
our lives differently, things would end any differently.
We have to trust the God of the Universe who directs
the outcome of all things that he will do that which
ultimately needs to be done.

—PATSY CLAIRMONT

A thousand years are but as yesterday to you!
They are like a single hour!

—PSALM 90:4 TLB

Anxiety springs from the desire that things should
happen as we wish rather than as God wills.

—ANONYMOUS

It is probably that Nature is not really in Time
and almost certain that God is not.

—C. S. LEWIS

There's a huge difference in the hands on our clock and God's.
Eternity for God is a never-ending present, says Saint Augustine
in the *Confessions*. "Thy [God's] years neither come nor go," he says,
"whereas ours both come and go, that they all may come." Go figure.
Truth is, we can't really comprehend how God sees time. Augustine
supposes it's sort of a past, present and future all in one view. But
suffice it to say, God's got the whole picture. We don't. We're bound
by time. God's not.

So why, when a decision looms, do we agonize, pace the floor,
drive ourselves loony with worrying? Why can't we just trust that
God's got the timing thing down pat? Why can't we pray for guidance, then hand it over?

Well, we do pray, and we do wait (a nanosecond), for God to show us the way. But in typical worrywart fashion, we can't seem to let go. So after we've supposedly given over our worries to God, we grab them back and start obsessing again. *Should we take the job now? Or should we wait? What if we take it and something better comes along? Are we being too cautious? Or not taking enough risk?* And on and on ad nauseam. We torture ourselves, playing the scenario over and over again in our minds, as though if we do that enough times, it will lead us to the right answer. We continue to fool ourselves, thinking we have the power to make everything turn out fine—if only we pick the right time.

Anxiety-ridden thinking often makes us act too quickly. And actions taken too soon can blow up in our faces. Like little children, we find it hard to trust our Parent's timing, so we whine. "Things are happening too fast, God. Why can't they slow down?" Or "Why aren't things happening faster, God?" The story of Abraham's wife, Sarah, is a classic example.

God promises Abraham his descendants will be harder to count than the stars in the sky. Naturally, he tells Sarah, and she starts stockpiling cloth for baby clothes. Yet, years go by and no children. Abraham, who's beginning to have doubts himself, tells Sarah to have patience, have faith. And outwardly Sarah does. But worrywarts like us can just imagine what was rattling around in her brain: *I've tried to be patient. I've tried to have faith. But let's face it, I'm no spring ewe anymore. God gave Abraham the descendants and the stars promise decades ago, and everyone has kids but us. If something doesn't happen soon, everything we have will go to a servant.*

So worrywart Sarah jumps the gun. She gives Hagar, her slave, to Abraham as a surrogate wife, opens up a proverbial can of worms and causes everyone a heap of pain and suffering. Of course, years later when things looked downright impossible (the Lord loves impossibilities), God delivers on his promise. Sarah gets pregnant, and as Genesis tells us, she "bore a son to Abraham in his old age *at the very time God had promised*" (emphasis mine). Abraham was one hundred and Sarah, ninety, and even she had to laugh, pat her belly and say the equivalent of "Who would have thunk it?"

Exactly. We never know how things are going to turn out. So why not have faith in the timing of the One who does? And faith, as Philip Yancey describes in his book *Disappointment with God*, "means believing in advance what will only make sense in reverse." So let's give it a try. Trust that timing, in God's hands, is perfect. Then, too, we could always remember Sarah, smiling as her wrinkled hand rocked her son's cradle, and focus on the lessons she learned the hard way: that "the Lord loves us," that he is leading us, that "everything is possible for him," that "everything that happens . . . happens at the time God chooses," and that, though it may sometimes be hard for us to realize, everything is working out the way it should.

PRAYER

Dear Lord,

Help me to refuse to get caught up in the timing worry mill. Remind me to look in hindsight at all the things I fretted over that were timed to perfection by you. Give me the courage to let go of my fears and the wisdom to stop thinking I can control outcomes if I wait or charge ahead. And when I'm at my wits' end, agonizing over when I should do something, let me remember Isaiah's words: "Whether you turn to the right or to the left, your ears will hear a voice behind you saying, 'This is the way; walk in it.'" Help me walk in your way, Lord, in peace and calmness.

◆ ◆ ◆

CHAPTER 21

A Sympathetic Ear

Hear, Oh LORD, and answer me, for I am . . . needy.
[When I'm in] trouble, I will call to you for you
will answer me.

—PSALM 86:1, 7

How often we look upon God as our last and feeblest
resource. We go to him because we have nowhere else to go.
And then we learn that the storms of life have driven us,
not upon the rocks, but into the desired haven.

—GEORGE MACDONALD

In my distress, I called to the LORD, and he answered me. . . .
I called for help, and you listened to my cry.

—JONAH 2:2

Can a mother forget the baby at her breast and
have no compassion on the child she has borne?
Though she may forget, I will not forget you!

—ISAIAH 49:15

If you tell your troubles to God, you put them into the
grave; they will never rise again, when you have committed
them to Him. If you roll your burden anywhere else, it will
roll back again, like the stone of Sisyphus.

—CHARLES HADDON SPURGEON

Before Kate married her fireman boyfriend, Jimmy, she seldom
got upset when he was a few minutes late. When they got married, though, her level of anxiety increased, and she was openly fidg-
ety until Jimmy walked in the door. One night when he got caught
in traffic and didn't call, she worked herself into such a frenzy, she
pounced on him as soon as he got home.

And that was just the start. Kate's bouts of anxiety began to
intensify and were filled with morbid images she couldn't seem to

shake. It was as if someone had turned on a horror film she couldn't turn off. She became excessively fearful, irritable and demanding, and the stress took its toll on her marriage. Then a friend of Kate's suggested she join a firemen's wives' support group. The first few weeks, she just observed. But then one night, the floodgates opened.

"I railed against my husband, the fire department, God, and then started blaming myself for being so weak and irrational. I must have talked nonstop for who knows how long. No one interrupted me or said I was overreacting or hysterical. They just listened. It was like a huge weight was lifted from my heart." But the climax of the evening for Kate was when one of the women asked her if she had ever talked to God like she had just talked to the group and let him in on her feelings. "He won't be offended, you know," she said. "He's heard worse. And besides," she reminded Kate, "he's a very good listener."

Admittedly, a sympathetic ear can work wonders when fear and anxiety get out of hand. People flock to self-help groups and psychologists' offices, not to mention bending friends' ears, for just that reason. Yet, we often forget we have another, more powerful, resource closer by. In fact, the best sympathetic ear and the One who can help us the most is God.

Sure . . . if we have grave anxieties. But we can't go running to God all the time with our annoying little fears . . . our petty complaints . . . or can we?

The Bible says, "Cast *all* [not some or only the really serious] anxiety on him because he cares for you." So it's obvious God is in for a penny or a pound. He wants us to come to him whenever we're nervous and fretful. He is ready and waiting for us to unburden ourselves. He wants us to depend on him. Whether it's something as compelling as Kate's problem or something much simpler, God wants us to talk things over with him, confide in him. God is always listening.

What's more, God wants us to talk to him regularly and not just in formal prayer on Sundays. Like Abraham, we can question him. Like Elijah, we can entreat him. Like Job, we can even vent and complain to him. God wants to hear it all. As a father shows his love for his child by listening when the child talks nonstop about the monster under the bed, so God wants to show his love by comforting us when we bring him our anxieties and troubles. And how pleased he must be when we place our childlike trust in him that way.

The Bible tells us we ought to "approach the throne of grace with confidence, so that we may receive mercy and find grace to help us in our time of need," an invitation for worrywarts to call on God, if ever there was one. Indeed, God never expects us to face fear alone. His "unfailing love" is our comfort. We can turn to him day or night. We can pour out our hearts to him. And we don't need an appointment. We need only call, and God will give us his undivided attention. He's all ears.

PRAYER

Dearest God,

*Your Son told us we're no longer "servants," we're "friends."
And friendship is built on trust. So please help me trust you first
and foremost with all my worries—real or imagined—from the
littlest to the most threatening. Teach me to turn to you instinc-
tively, like a chick to its mother, at the first hint of fear, depend
on you and not everyone but (or then) you for my solace, and
talk to you often from morning until night about anything and
everything, the way good friends always do. Oh, and, Lord, when
it's my turn, remind me to listen politely, while the wisdom of
your divine conversation fills my soul.*

◆ ◆ ◆

CHAPTER 22

Limiting Others' Lives

To love anyone is nothing else than to
wish that person good.

—SAINT THOMAS AQUINAS

Love seeks not limits but outlets.

—ANONYMOUS

We never know how much one loves till we know how
much he is willing to endure and suffer for us.

—HENRY WARD BEECHER

I am he, I am he who will sustain you.
I have made you and I will carry you.
I will sustain you and I will rescue you.

—ISAIAH 46:4

Wheresoever a man seeketh his own,
there he falleth from love.

—THOMAS À KEMPIS

Those who wish to transform the world must
learn to transform themselves.

—KONRAD HEIDEN

*C*harlie was on vacation with his wife, and they stumbled onto a bakery with signs in the window for all sorts of mouthwatering breads. They both loved bread, so they went inside.

"Go ahead, Charlie, pick one, any one, and I'll pay for it," his wife urged sweetly.

Charlie examined his choices, then finally picked a crusty Italian bread, stuffed with bits of provolone cheese, prosciutto ham and olives baked into it.

"I like this one," he said to his wife.

His wife picked up the bread, mentally tallied up the calories, then put it back on the shelf.

"No, you don't, Charlie," she said, handing him a dry low-calorie whole wheat.

"You don't like that one, you like this one."

A worrywart always knows what's best for their loved ones. That's because we're vigilant caretakers who are more aware than most that this nasty world is replete with all sorts of evil, sickness, danger, not to mention calories and other hurtful and downright deadly stuff lurking in every corner—reason aplenty for us to get apoplectic just thinking about people we care for adrift in it. If we could, we'd shove them into a protective ziplock bag and carry them around in our pockets all day. We can't. So we do the next best thing: like Chicken Little, we run around all aflutter, trying to push them out of the way of the falling sky.

We fuss about their feelings, their business trips, ingrown toenails, digestion and dandruff. Murphy's law, we figure, anything that could go wrong with them will. That is—unless *we* step in and take action. So we micromanage their lives, trying to limit their exposure to what we perceive as dangerous or unwise. We do this by coercing and manipulating. "Don't go there," we plead. "I *worry* so when you do. You're *driving* on the interstate? I won't sleep a wink. Pizza? With pepperoni *and all* that cheese? Oh my!" Of course, we only do this . . . because we love them.

But is it really love? Or are we afraid? Afraid we can't bear the pain if they get hurt; afraid we'll totally fall apart and won't be strong for them; afraid we'll despair; afraid we'll lose our faith in God, his plan, ourselves. The Bible says fear and love can't coexist because "perfect love drives out fear." It also says "love is not selfish"; it "is never irritable"; and it "always trusts." So rather than controlling, real love liberates. It seeks to free people to experience a full life—one with both ups and downs. If we truly love someone, we allow them to become the person they were meant to be so they can fulfill the purpose God set out for them—a purpose that may or may not correspond with our view of what's good for them.

Take Lazarus, for example. Jesus loved Lazarus and didn't want him to die. But he didn't butt in or try to manipulate the situation. He didn't say, "Friend, you're looking a bit piqued. You had better eat your spinach; take some vitamins. You're worrying me. Maybe I'd better stay and look after you." Instead, Jesus left town as planned, and when he heard that Lazarus was "very, very sick," he stayed away two more days—two more agonizing days, which probably ripped his heart out. But he knew his Father had a plan, and he wasn't about to interfere with it, even if it would make him feel better, even if it meant he would have to see his friends suffer.

That's an example of the kind of love Jesus is talking about when he says, "Love one another as I have loved you."

Difficult? You bet. But it's doable. Jesus proved that. And since he's been there and knows exactly how it feels, he can sympathize when we pray to him to give us strength. So why not ask him to help us control our controlling selves, so we can show our loved ones real love by allowing them to live their own lives, make their own decisions, experience joy, pain, discouragement (choose their own bread) and anything else that's necessary for them to learn and grow. Let's ask him to teach us that, though we'd love to run and catch them, we have to let the people we love stumble and fall. In this way, they can get back up, and without any nudging from us, go on to choose the best path into their Father's arms.

PRAYER

Dearest God,

I know I drive people crazy by obsessively worrying about them. I know I have to leave them alone to make their own decisions. I know I have to stop using my fears to manipulate them into doing things they don't want to do. There, I've said it. Now, I just need to act on it. That's where you come in, God. Please help me to detach with love from the ones I love, and leave them in your protective care. You know what's best for them so much more than I do. So I pray that your will be done, not mine. Help me to love them in a way that will be supportive without stifling, encouraging without overpowering and concerned but not controlling. Lord, I pray you'll lead them in your ways and keep them safely under your wing.

◆ ◆ ◆

CHAPTER 23

Angels Abounding

Make yourself familiar with the angels, and behold
them frequently in spirit; for without being seen,
they are present with you.

—SAINT FRANCIS DE SALES

Every visible thing in this world is put in the
charge of an angel.

—SAINT AUGUSTINE

The guardian angels of life sometimes fly so high as to be
beyond our sight, but they are always looking down upon us.

—JEAN PAUL RICHTER

Then he [Jacob] dreamed, and behold, a ladder was set up
on the earth, and its top reached to heaven; and there the
angels of God were ascending and descending on it.

—GENESIS 28:12

All God's angels come to us disguised.

—JAMES RUSSELL LOWELL

Behold, I send an angel before you, to guard you on the way
and to bring you to the place which I have prepared. Give
heed to him and hearken to his voice. . . .

—EXODUS 23:20–21

T he thunder and lightning woke Vicky up. She knew how her
six-year-old, Jason, hated storms, so she peeked in to see if he
was okay.

"I know it's silly to be frightened, but I can't help it," she heard a
voice say. "It's pretty loud down here." The words were coming from
a big lump in the middle of the bed, which Vicky recognized as Jason
huddled in the center under the covers.

"So, how much longer?" Jason asked.

Vicky turned on the light and walked over to the bed.

"Jason, honey, it's Mom. Who are you talking to?" she asked
gently.

"My guardian angel," Jason answered. "Someone at school told me thunder is the angels bowling and lightning is them taking pictures. So I was just asking my angel how much longer they're going to be at it."

Remember how good it felt to talk to our guardian angels? When we were little kids, we turned to them often when we felt frightened or in need of protection. And in return for our faith and trust, God rewarded us with a sense of well-being and comfort we'd give anything to recapture today.

The good news is our angels haven't gone anywhere. And though some of us probably haven't had a heart-to-heart with them in a couple of decades, that doesn't mean they've forgotten us. The Bible says if we trust God, he'll order his angels "to guard" us so "no harm will befall" us or "no disaster will come near. . . ." It also says God promises his angels will lift us "up in their hands," so we won't as much as strike our "foot against a stone." And all that is gratis—regardless of whether we have chats with them on a routine basis or not.

Ironically, now that we're older and have drifted away from our childlike dependence, our angels are probably as busy or busier than ever—helping us make decisions, getting us out of scrapes, protecting us from bodily harm, talking us through uncertainties, and fighting off evil demons bent on tricking us into sin and danger. Though they seldom leave calling cards, if we checked, we'd probably see their handiwork daily in countless incidents that rescue us—like the time we left our pocketbooks with all manner of credit cards, not to mention a king's ransom in makeup, in the grocery parking lot, only to have it hung on our doors by a stranger (angel?), or the near disaster when our shoes caught on our jeans and we slipped down a whole flight of stairs without hurting anything but our pride.

And while the part they play in our lives may not be as flashy and obvious as angels of old—angels like the one who stepped in to stop Abraham from sacrificing his son, the ones who saved Daniel from ravenous lions and protected Shadrach, Meshach and Abednego from the fiery furnace, the one who single-handedly wiped out "185,000 Assyrian troops" or the one who used his get-out-of-jail card to rescue Paul—still we could not fight the good fight without them. Goodness knows what state we'd be in if they were not only there to divert us from bodily harm, but also to distract us from worries that would probably keep us in a tailspin for days.

Indeed, all angels are hypersensitive to the fact that we mortals are nervous wrecks, which is probably why in Jesus's time, the first thing out of their mouths wasn't "Hello" or "How are you?" but "Do not worry" or "Be not afraid." So we know they recognize we have a huge problem with anxiety, and they stand ready to do what they can to help us over it.

So let's let them. Let's renew our childhood friendships with the angels and make them an important part of our lives. Let's ask them to help us fight fear and anxiety so we can serve God better and have greater faith in his plan. Let's keep mental images of angels in our minds and hearts and be on the lookout for their help in the kindness of a stranger. The Bible says we have often "entertained angels without knowing it." So let's bear that in mind when we're tempted to be short or blasé with people who come our way. After all, we never know who sent them.

PRAYER

Dearest God,

Thank you for making angels and for giving them the patience they have. My angel must really be something. Down through the years, I'd imagine she's had quite a time of it—what with all the inane, dangerous and downright sinful things I had to be steered away from—not to mention all the times she calmed me down when I got fits of nervous prostration. Help me to be mindful of this powerful ally you've given me, and give me the grace to listen to her voice of reason when I'm caught on the worry-go-round. Lord, open my eyes to the angel right next to me, so I can get a better view of the angels all around.

◆ ◆ ◆

CHAPTER 24

Attitude of Gratitude

Some people complain because God put thorns on roses,
while others praise Him for putting roses among thorns.

—ANONYMOUS

I will give thanks to the LORD.

—PSALM 7:17

Do not be anxious about anything, but in everything,
by prayer and petition, with thanksgiving, present your
requests to God. And the peace of God, which transcends

all understanding, will guard your hearts and your
minds in Christ Jesus.

—PHILIPPIANS 4:6, 7

God's will is determined by His wisdom which always
perceives, and His goodness which always embraces,
the intrinsically good.

—C. S. LEWIS

As antitoxins prevent the disastrous effects of certain
poisons and diseases, thanksgiving destroys the poison of
faultfinding [worry] and grumbling. When trouble has
smitten us, a spirit of thanksgiving is a soothing antiseptic.

—CLINTON C. COX

Thou who hast given so much to me, give one thing more,
a grateful heart, for Christ's sake.

—GEORGE HERBERT

T hank you, God" is a sentence worrywarts ought to say
frequently—from the time we wake up to the time we lay our
heads on the pillows. An attitude of gratitude casts out fear and
worry and reminds us how gracious our God is and how fortunate

(or as the thesaurus puts it, "blessed," "out in front," "ahead of the game," "golden," "favored" and "well-off") we are to be his children, showered with his grace, love and protection. Saying thank you shows God we have faith in his Providence, and believe, as the Bible tells us, that he "will not forsake" us, but will "protect" us and "guard" us always. And if that's the case, why feel agitated and anxious?

The Bible tells us we should "give thanks in all circumstances," and if only we can develop that habit, nothing that comes our way can throw us—because we'll approach all situations as experiences a loving God is sending our way. The Bible says, "God's faithful love endures forever!" And a loving God wouldn't send us anything that in the long run wouldn't be to our benefit.

Yet, it's hard to say "Thank you, God" when situations appear hopeless, unless we train ourselves to count our blessings no matter what. The Bible tells us to "give thanks to the LORD," and "remember the wonders he has done," and recalling those memories—the blessings he's given us and the trials he's helped us with in the past (the ones we thought we'd never get through)—can remind us to trust him in any situation—in the present.

Jonah had to learn that lesson fast. From his viewpoint, it would have appeared things were regressing from bad—being thrown into an angry sea—to worse—being eaten by a huge fish. Now even though Jonah knew he deserved punishment for disobeying God, he called on the Lord to deliver him from drowning. And while being gulped down by a big fish probably wasn't what he had in mind as a solution, he believed God heard his prayer and saved him. So, once inside the fish, rather than eating himself up (sorry) with worry or questioning God's modus operandi, Jonah immediately said, "How can I thank you enough for all you have done?" giving God praise and credit for rescuing him, which as it turns out was exactly the case.

Indeed, facing each moment with an attitude of gratitude transforms our lives, giving us a healthier perspective. It forces us to see the glass half full instead of half empty. If we say, "Thank you, God" for getting me to work safely, we can't stay focused on the guy who ran the stop sign and nearly hit us. If we say, "Thank you, God" for giving me a job when lots of people are out of work, it helps take our minds off a less-than-perfect boss. If we say, "Thank you, God" for my wonderful house, it will stop us worrying about the garage that needs painting.

Our goal is to get to the point where "Thank you, God," not "Oh, my God!" becomes our automatic response to any and every situation that arises, even when we can't imagine what good can possibly come of it. This way, like Jonah, we can look at anything—a humongous fish or a toothache—as a blessing in disguise. (Hey, even a toothache can be a godsend if it stops us eating candy and helps us rid ourselves of five pounds.) So let's remember to keep "Thank you, God" on our lips and an attitude of gratitude in our hearts so we can, as the Bible suggests, "always give thanks for *everything* to God the Father."

PRAYER

Dearest God,

When I look back at all the blessings you've given me in my life, and how you've always been there for me, I marvel that I wound up being such a worrywart. But I've only one thing to say about that: "Thank you, God." Whatever the reason, I trust my being a worrywart will ultimately serve your purpose. So, though I struggle with this problem, I trust you to either help me bear or help me banish it. Either way, I praise you for your love and kindness.

◆ ◆ ◆

CHAPTER 25

Prayer, Practice, Pretending

There are no miracles to men who don't believe in them.

—ANONYMOUS

Say you are well, or all is well with you, and God
shall hear your words and make them true.

—ELLA WHEELER WILCOX

The promises of God are certain, but they do not
all mature in ninety days.

—ADONIRAM J. GORDON

Trust in God and do something.

—MARY LYON

Be joyful in hope, patient in affliction, faithful in prayer.

—ROMANS 12:12

He is a shield for all who take refuge in him.

—PSALM 18:30

I sought the LORD and . . . he delivered me
from all my fears.

—PSALM 34:4

When I am afraid, I will trust in you.

—PSALM 56:3

Fear and trembling have beset me; horror has overwhelmed
me. But I call to God, and the LORD saves me.

—PSALM 55:5, 16

Ever wanted to be an actress? If you're a worrywart, now's your time to try. Acting "as if" we're not anxious when, in fact, we really are, temporarily interrupts the cycle of worry so we can practice trusting God while we go about our business, uncomfortable, but functioning nonetheless. Then, after we survive a series of nail-biting experiences that turn out to be just as the Lord had planned them—nothing to worry about, the tiny voice in our heads will say, "See, I told you to trust God." Do this enough, and over time we'll be exchanging a nasty worry habit with a God-trusting one.

Truth is, we're not all born pillars of faith. Trust in God has to mature. And even then, no one is perfect. We *want* to believe, and we know we should. But until our faith grows, like the father who brought his son to Jesus to be cured, we keep telling God, "I do have faith, but not enough. Help me have more!" And one way to keep from being paralyzed by anxiety in the meantime while we wait is to continue to pray—and then pretend as if our prayers have already been answered.

The Bible says, "Faith by itself, if it is not accompanied by *action*, is dead," and "You see that a person is justified by what he *does* and not by faith alone" (emphases mine). Well, in this case, acting "as if" is our action plan, what we're doing, the viable step we're taking to conquer worry and make a strong faith a reality. We pretend to be calm and confident outside, even though inside we are a bundle of nerves. Obviously, God knows we're still anxious. But if he sees us trying something—anything—to get us moving in the right direction, he'll certainly applaud and reward our efforts.

God understands we can't always muster the faith we need to quit worrying right away. He understands we're weak. But Jesus says, "My power is made perfect in weakness." And Paul gives us an insight as to why, when he tells us what happened to him in Asia. "We were under great pressure . . .," he says. "But this happened that we might not rely on ourselves, but on God." See, God wants us to depend on him. He wants us to lean on him for help. And for all we know, he might just have given us this worry handicap on purpose, so that our search for ways to overcome it would lead us to grow closer to him.

So let's try this new strategy the next time we're tempted to give in to worry. À la Meryl Streep or Gwyneth Paltrow, let's give an award-winning performance, acting as if we're fine. Let's tell God and ourselves that we're going to practice having the strongest faith ever, that whatever happens will be the will of the Father Almighty, so it has to be okay, and that we're going to go about our lives as if anxiety wasn't the thorn in our sides that it really is.

PRAYER

Heavenly Father,

When it comes to trusting you completely, I'll admit, I'm a ninety-pound weakling. I've got a lot of faith-building work to do. Help me exercise my soul every chance I get so that one day, I won't have to pretend anymore. I long for the day I can say, "Lord, I know you're taking care of this, so I'm not worried." In the meantime, I depend on you to help me manage my anxieties so I can get on with my life. In Jesus's name, I thank you.

◆　◆　◆

CHAPTER 26

Real Success

[A]ll achievement springs from man's envy of
his neighbor. This, too, is meaningless, a
chasing after the wind.

—ECCLESIASTES 4:4

God will estimate success one day.

—ROBERT BROWNING

No other animal admires another animal.

—BLAISE PASCAL

[T]o accept his lot and be happy in his work—
this is a gift of God.

—ECCLESIASTES 5:19

Only in God does life have meaning and true pleasure.
Without him nothing satisfies. . . .

—NOTE ON ECCLESIASTES 2:24–25 in NIV

As long as he sought the LORD, God gave him success.

—2 CHRONICLES 26:5

Whatever you do, do it all for the glory of God.

—1 CORINTHIANS 10:31

Try not to become a man of success but rather
try to become a man of value.

—ALBERT EINSTEIN

Everyone loves a success story. Whether it's a mom-and-pop business that suddenly makes it big or a persistent singer who finally cuts a hit CD, we applaud people who "make it." They've captured that brass ring of achievement we are all taught from childhood to grab for. And they're enjoying the spoils—the wealth, prestige, glamour and recognition that go along with it. These are the people we emulate, the ones we want to be. Their successes are what motivates us. We want to be winners, too.

So, as per usual, we make ourselves crazy, as we take examples of people who've succeeded (in the world's eyes), and hold them up as benchmarks for us to compare ourselves to. *Why can't I be like Oprah Winfrey or Bill Gates or Jane Jones, our company's vice president?* we ask ourselves. Big mistake. Galatians tells us, "Be sure to do what you should, for then you will enjoy the personal satisfaction of having done your work well, and you won't need to compare yourself to anyone else." You see, God doesn't want us comparing our lives to others. He gave us a one-of-a-kind makeup, background and skill set for a reason. He has a purpose in mind for us and wants us to use what he gives us to be a success at being ourselves—not a frustrated imitation of someone else.

What's more, it's no secret: earthly success is fleeting. One day we are dot.comers with a Ferrari and houses in three countries. The next we're dot.goners, living in a walk-up and busing it to the unemployment office. And the funny part is, as much as we feel that not making it is the pits, somehow success isn't all it's cracked up to be, either. It never quite makes us as happy as we thought it would. After the first rush of excitement, there always seems to be something missing, a kind of hollow, empty feeling that says, "Okay, now what?"

Equally worrisome is success's addictive nature. Get one taste and we're always looking for more. The great composer Irving Berlin wasn't kidding when he said, "The toughest thing about success is that you've got to keep on being a success." So, though we should be satisfied, we can't rest on our laurels. We keep pushing ahead. One promotion is nice, two is outstanding. And, well, three proves we're no flash in the pan. Still, like chewing gum, the sweetness always seems to fade quickly, leaving a stale, rubbery feeling in our souls.

And talk about fickle! People go from hero to zero in a blink. Just as soon as someone else does something better or smarter, our successes are forgotten. Or if our beauty fades, our voices falter, the stocks slump or we can't run the race like we used to—when our hands are shaky and we can't hit the bull's-eye—the world pushes us aside and brushes off the seat for another achiever to take our places. Remember what's her name? they'll say. And what's his name? Wasn't he a bigwig at whatchamacallit?

Indeed, success always looks better from the outside looking in. And though most people are lucky to have Andy Warhol's fifteen minutes of fame (Andy who?), that doesn't stop us from craving it. So it looks like as long as our value system is stuck on being a winner in the eyes of this world, we're in for a heap of worry.

On the other hand, if we're open to it, real success is available to us, hassle free, every second of every day, no matter where we are or what we do. And the formula for achieving it is as easy as doing everything (from feeding a baby to presenting a budget) in Jesus's name and for the glory of God. The Bible says, "Commit to the LORD whatever you do and your plans will succeed." So it's not so much what we do, but how we do it that makes us memorable in God's eyes. And it's not so much what we are, senator or salesman, supermodel or stay-at-home mom, but what *kind* of salesman, senator, supermodel or stay-at-home mom we are that he takes into account.

Paul had the right idea when it comes to success. It's a savvy recipe that is summed up in two sentences from his letters to the Colossians. "*Whatever* you do," he said, "work at it with all your heart, as though *working for the Lord, not for men*, since you know you will receive an inheritance from the Lord as a reward" (emphases mine). If we go about our business with this in mind—that we're working for God, not men—we won't worry or get our whiskers out of whack about promotions or accolades because we'll have our sights set higher. Instead of climbing the here-today-gone-tomorrow corporate ladder, or having our names up in lights, we'll discover the real meaning of success, the golden parachute God offers: being with him, in heaven, forever and ever.

PRAYER

Dearest Father,

*I*s *there anyone more ungrateful than I am? Probably not. Instead of thanking you for the successes you've given me, I'm always grousing about what I don't have. I see others "getting ahead," and I'm envious. Even though I have so much as it is, I'm not satisfied. I want it all. Remind me, Lord, how short-lived and hollow earthly success is, and how foolish I am to let vainglory jeopardize eternal life with you. Help me remember that being a winner in your eyes is what's important, and that if I do every-thing for your glory, not my own, I'll have a shot—not at a measly corner office—but at one of those rooms in heaven your Son is preparing for me.*

◆ ◆ ◆

CHAPTER 27

Do not repay anyone evil for evil.

—ROMANS 12:17

Trying to get even spreads evil. We might say that in
this respect evil is like poison ivy; the more you scratch,
the more it itches, and the more it spreads.

—A. NICHOLS

Nothing in this lost and ruined world bears the meek
impress of the Son of God so surely as forgiveness.

—ALICE CARY

Then Peter came to Jesus and asked, "Lord, how many times shall I forgive my brother when he sins against me? Up to seven times?" Jesus answered, "I tell you, not seven times, but seventy times seven."

—MATTHEW 18:21–22

There is no use talking as if forgiveness were easy.

—C. S. LEWIS

And forgive us our sins, just as we have forgiven those who have sinned against us.

—MATTHEW 6:12 TLB

Every day in every way our senses get bombarded with regular doses of evil. War, business fraud, famine and genocide have become commonplace. And what used to be unimaginable horrors—like mothers leaving babies in Dumpsters to die, children mowing down classmates who rub them the wrong way and terrorists systematically obliterating thousands of lives in a heartbeat—have become frightening realities. It's the stuff of sensationalist tabloids. Only it's real. And that's what makes it so surreal and so worrisome.

Getting anxious over evil won't make it go away, though. Instead, we need to mount an all-out offensive, using Jesus and his teachings as our ammunition. A vacationer from Asia did just that eight years ago. Her story still sticks in my mind after all this time because she acted so out of character with our violent and vengeful society; she left me in tears. Here's how the six o'clock news reported the incident.

Kim, we'll call her, was rushing to catch a subway in New York City and bumped into another woman—nothing malicious—just a case of being in a hurry. Taking this as a personal affront, the other woman went on the attack. She followed Kim into the train, took a box cutter and slashed her face. The resultant gaping hole required over twenty-five stitches to close. Afterward, as Kim left the hospital, a newscaster asked her the quintessential reporter's question: "How do you feel about what happened?" then stood back expecting an emotional tirade of anger.

What occurred next was truly a miracle—a triumph of good over evil, if ever there was one. With a bandage obliterating half her face, Kim, who was young and very attractive, announced through an interpreter that *she* was sorry. She said she did not mean to bump into her attacker. She said she forgave her for what she had done. She said she would pray for her. She said she felt sorry that in a city of so many people, her attacker felt so little love.

Not what we'd expect. No lashing out at the mayor. Or the police. Or the woman who most likely scarred her for life—all of which would have been understandable under the circumstances. Kim didn't spew hatred or involve race. She didn't cry. She wasn't bitter. She didn't feel sorry for herself. She just stood there, bearing her pain, and forgave.

Kim's forgiveness was instant and complete, and accomplished two things: It made it easier for her to accept what happened, put it in the past and get on with healing, and it stopped dead in its tracks the evil visited on her. With dignity and unbelievable selflessness, she suffered the bad, absorbed it and defused it, robbing it of its energy to get free, escalate and strike again.

Kim didn't say she was a Christian. It didn't come up. Yet she showed everyone who saw her she was truly a Christlike person willing to fight evil with the only weapons that work: forgiveness and love. Putting the lesson of the cross into practice seemed second-nature for her. It was as though Jesus himself, speaking through her, was addressing viewers like me watching the news. And if we listened closely, we could hear him say, "This is the way to beat evil: forgive, as I have forgiven you."

God willing, we will never be called on to fight evil on such a grand scale. But we face smaller battles—ego-shattering incidents of insults, gossip, lies, mean-spiritedness, prejudice—which are thrown in our paths every day. Turning the other cheek when someone talks down to us or is rude is never easy. But if, like Kim, we're ever going to send evil packing, we are going to have to keep working on it. The Bible says we "can do all things through Christ who strengthens" us. So let's stop worrying about evil and, instead, start fighting it tooth and nail. With Jesus as our commander and brave soldiers like Kim to lead us by their example, we can't lose.

PRAYER

Dear Jesus,

No evil could be worse than what happened to you. Yet you forgave. You showed us how to overcome the worst. So why, when my injuries are so trivial, do I have such trouble letting things go? Help me, Lord, remember the insults, the lies, the scourging, the excruciating pain you, who are blameless, suffered on my account. Strengthen me so I can overlook petty blows and not hold grudges. Help me show everyone by my example that the best way to deal with evil is to shine love in its face and overwhelm it with forgiveness.

◆ ◆ ◆

CHAPTER 28

Your Father Always Loves You

The unfailing love of the LORD never ends! . . .
Great is his faithfulness; his mercies begin afresh each day.

—LAMENTATIONS 3:22, 23

Trying to build the brotherhood of man without
the fatherhood of God is like trying to make a
wheel without a hub.

—IRENE DUNN

God, Thou art love! I build my faith on that.

—ROBERT BROWNING

Love is an image of God, and not a lifeless image,
but the living essence of the divine nature which
beams full of all goodness.

—MARTIN LUTHER

The greatest happiness of life is the conviction
that we are loved—loved for ourselves, or rather,
loved in spite of ourselves.

—VICTOR HUGO

Though our feelings come and go, His love for us does not.
It is not wearied by our sins, or our indifference; and,
therefore, it is quite relentless in its determination that
we shall be cured of those sins, at whatever cost to us,
at whatever cost to Him.

—C. S. LEWIS

When we worry and fuss, we act as though God doesn't exist. But he loves us anyway. Isn't that amazing?

God's love is so amazing, it's hard to fathom in human terms. So we tend to saddle him with our own notions about love. For us, love can be here today, gone tomorrow. God's love is constant. We're always worrying about whether this one or that one loves us. We never have to with God. We can have a fight with someone and, for a time, not love them. Impossible for God. The Bible says, "Nothing can ever separate us from (God's) love. Death can't, and life can't. The angels can't, and the demons can't. Our fears for today, our worries about tomorrow and even the powers of hell can't keep God's love away." That's a pretty powerful statement.

But not when we consider that's what God had planned in the first place. The Bible says, "Long ago, even before he made the world, God loved us and chose us. . . . His unchanging plan has always been to adopt us into his own family. . . ." So he loved us before we even were "us."

And now that we've grown into anxious adults, God loves us just the same. Nothing has changed, nor can it. He loves us even when we act like he's not around. Take the time the disciples lost it in the boat when a sudden storm arose. They had God, in the flesh, right with them, but they were petrified just the same. So much so, they had to go wake him up. And Jesus calmed the seas for them.

Though we let our anxieties keep God at arm's length, he doesn't let worry keep him from us. He never gets angry with us or frustrated; he never says, "That's it, I'm finished." He never calls us ungrateful or silly or disloyal, though we are all of that and more. And even though we don't listen to him when he tells us not to worry, and even though we act as though he doesn't have power over our worries, he never quits. The Bible says, "He remember(s) our utter weaknesses, for his loving-kindness continues forever." God's "unfailing" love never gives up. He will always seek out the lost sheep; always welcome back the prodigal son; always be there for us—no matter what.

PRAYER

Dearest Jesus,

Sometimes it blows my mind that you could love someone as thick as me. I mean, how many times do I have to hear you say, "Don't worry," before it sinks in? How can I believe you really love me when I keep getting as anxious as I do? Strengthen my will, Lord, so I can fight off these persistent worry demons; open my mind, Lord, so I can think loving thoughts of you, and teach my heart, Lord, to trust in your amazing love.

◆ ◆ ◆

CHAPTER 29

Reining In Imagination

How much pain have cost us the evils which
have never happened!

—THOMAS JEFFERSON

Worry, the interest paid by those who borrow trouble.

—GEORGE WASHINGTON LYON

Our life is what our thoughts make it.

—MARCUS AURELIUS

Do not fret—it leads only to evil.

—PSALM 37:8

Present fears are less than horrible imaginings.

—WILLIAM SHAKESPEARE

We walk in circles, so limited by our own anxieties
that we can no longer distinguish between true
and false. . . .

—INGMAR BERGMAN

There are more things, Lucilius, that frighten us
than injure us, and we suffer more in imagination
than in reality.

—SENECA

We are, perhaps uniquely among the earth's creatures,
the worrying animal. We worry away our lives,
fearing the future, discontent with the present,
unable to take in the idea of dying, unable to sit still.

—LEWIS THOMAS

*H*ere's a paraphrased modern-day parable from Father Anthony de Mello about imaginary worries. Can you guess who the tenth camel is?

Some men who were herding camels stopped one night in the desert. The youngest went to his master with a problem. "We have ten camels, but only nine pegs. What should I do?" The master scratched his beard, then he answered, "These camels are pretty gullible animals. Pretend to tie the tenth camel up, and he won't know the difference." So the young herder did just that, and the camel stayed. However, in the morning, when all the other camels were ready to go, the tenth camel wouldn't budge. The young herder went to the master again and told him what was going on. "Well," said the master, "did you untie him?" The young man looked at the master blankly. Then he went back and went through the motions of untying the camel. Lo and behold, the camel immediately followed the pack.

We worriers are like the tenth camel. We're tied to imaginary pegs of anxiety, and the devil couldn't be happier. Some anonymous wise man said it all with this aphorism: "The devil would have us continually crossing streams that do not exist."

Yup, the devil loves to pull the wool over our eyes. He likes nothing better than that we spend precious time in an irrational flux over nothing. That leaves us less time for God. Jesus calls Satan the "father of lies" and tells us lies are Satan's "native language." He uses them as smoke and mirrors to get worriers all aflutter. The worrisome thoughts he's putting in our heads are things that aren't so— they're lies—things that will never happen.

On the other hand, we can't lump all our concerns into a basket marked "bogus". We have to, as the Bible advises, "examine everything carefully and hold fast to that which is good," which means focusing on a concern long enough to ask ourselves a few questions (*What am I worrying about? What are the chances it will occur? Can I do anything about it this very minute?*), make a decision, act on it, then let the worry go. So, for instance, if we cut ourselves on an old rusty nail and worry that the cut might get infected, and that worry pushes us to go to an emergency room to have it seen to, we've benefited. However, if we go to the emergency room, have the cut dressed, get a tetanus shot, then, because we get a twinge, start to have irrational thoughts of our foot swelling up, getting gangrene and having our leg cut off at the knee—well, guess who's using our imaginations to deceive us, to get us caught up in lies?

Worriers have good imaginations. It's part of our problem. But it can be part of our solution, too. Just as we can visualize a bad outcome that has very little or no possibility of happening, we can ask God for the grace to dismiss it quickly, then imagine a good outcome, one that is far more likely to happen because God loves us.

So when the devil gets up to his tricks again, let's pray for clarity to rationally distinguish the fake ties that bind us to imaginary pegs, and the real problems we can do something about. Our Heavenly Father has visualized only good things for us from before we were even created. So let's have faith in him and imagine them for ourselves, too.

PRAYER

Heavenly Father,

The great deceiver is very slick. He lies to me, preys on my fears and stirs up anxieties, so that every molehill becomes a mountain and every pimple a tumor. With your help, Lord, I can dismiss him and his unrealistic nonsense quickly. Teach me to see through his charade at the onset, so I can look at whatever comes to me—in a peaceful, rational way—knowing that my Father wants only the best for me.

◆ ◆ ◆

CHAPTER 30

Two Worrisome Words

The tongue also is a fire, a world of evil among the parts of the body.

—JAMES 3:6

Therefore each of you must put off falsehood and speak truthfully to his neighbor, for we are all members of one body.

—EPHESIANS 4:25

There is no more miserable human being than one in whom nothing is habitual but indecision.

—WILLIAM JAMES

For one's own peace of mind, I think it is best to
set a time limit for one's decisions.

—C. S. LEWIS

Whatever Heaven ordains is best.

—CONFUCIUS

I know, O LORD, that a man's life is not his own;
it is not for man to direct his steps.

—JEREMIAH 10:23

Trust in the LORD with all your heart and lean not
on your own understanding. In all your ways acknowledge
him, and he will make your paths straight.

—PROVERBS 3:5, 6

Who would have thought when my mother taught me the words "yes" and "no" they'd cause me so much anxiety? Oh, not when I was a kid. Things were much simpler then. I had no worries because when I said "yes" or "no," I meant just that. Even better, my limited vocabulary assured everyone there would be no barrage of excuses to follow. My childish approach probably caused my parents (and myself) some embarrassment on occasion. But

God approved of my straightforwardness. And it wouldn't surprise me if he wasn't sad to see me grow up and out of it.

The word "no" just seems to stick in my craw. It's so short. So curt. So final. There's no wiggle room in a "no." It's like a door slamming shut. It seems rude, uncivilized, unfriendly. ("Maybe" is much more pliable.) So, for example, when someone asks me if I want to go somewhere or do something, or if I like something or don't, I often catch myself saying "yes" when that's not what I want to say.

I did this once with my best friend. We were on vacation and at the beach. I had had enough sun, and she had, too. But we each were worried that the other wanted to stay. So out of what we thought was concern for the other person, we both got burned to a crisp—because neither of us wanted to say "no."

You'd think I'd learn. Yet I continue to have trouble saying "no" because I worry I'll hurt someone's feelings; I'll make a bad impression; people won't like me; I won't fit in, whatever. And it's really inane, because whether I want to admit it or not, when I don't say what I mean, I'm not being honest. I'm lying. And down the line, more often than not, the truth outs, and my dishonesty winds up offending everybody. The result is that people lose faith in me. They don't trust what I say. And neither do I. Worse still, I'm getting in hot water with God. Talk about a lose-lose situation.

The Bible says that "truth stands the test of time; lies are soon exposed"; that "a good man's mind is filled with honest thoughts; an evil man's mind is crammed with lies," and that "lies will get any man into trouble, but honesty is its own defense." It also warns us that the tongue "corrupts the whole person, sets the whole course of his life on fire, and is itself set on fire by hell." That's certainly an incentive to quit worrying and do something fast. If it means standing in front of a mirror every night and saying "no" fifty times until I can say it without a hitch, I'd better get to it.

The Bible also tells me to "direct my footsteps according to [God's] word." And when I do, wouldn't you know, it's all spelled out in black and white for me. Here's what Jesus says on the subject, and it couldn't be plainer: "Just say 'Yes' or 'No,'" he tells us flat out. "Anything else you say comes from the Evil One."

Certainly, "no" is the one word I want to be able to shoot from the hip with when Satan's around. And I have to be quick on the draw. Because if I falter, even for a minute, I know the devil will come in for the kill. Jesus was a sharpshooter with his "no's." He never even had to say the word. He used Scripture instead. When the devil tempted him in the desert—"If you are the Son of God, tell these stones to become bread"—Jesus shot right back, "It is written, 'Man does not live on bread alone, but on every word that comes from the mouth of God.'" No waffling here. Jesus was an expert at saying "no"—to temptation, to riches, to power, to the Pharisees' hypocrisy, to the old ways, even to his disciples when they were on the wrong track about something. He never put people's feelings before his Father's. He didn't care if he was popular. He wasn't worried about offending anyone. I shouldn't worry either—especially since there's so much at stake.

PRAYER

Dearest Jesus,

Help me quit being wishy-washy when it comes to saying "yes" and "no." Rather, teach me to say what I mean and mean what I say so I can live a life of integrity, one that's pleasing to you. Remind me also that I should approach life's question marks in the knowledge that, with you beside me, I'm being led to make right decisions.

◆ ◆ ◆

CHAPTER 31

What's Done Is Done

Make the least of what goes and the most of what comes.

—ANONYMOUS

The Moving Finger writes; and, having writ,
Moves on: nor all your Piety nor Wit
Shall lure it back to cancel half a Line,
Nor all your tears wash out a Word of it.

—THE RUBÁIYÁT OF OMAR KHAYYÁM

Things without remedy should be without regard;
what's done is done.

—WILLIAM SHAKESPEARE

He seldom reflects on the days of his life because
God keeps him occupied with gladness of heart.
—ECCLESIASTES 5:20

Only by acceptance of the past, can you alter it.
—T. S. ELIOT

Always look at what you have left. Never look at
what you have lost.
—ROBERT H. SCHULLER

If a stranger tried to rob us of our todays by forcing us to think
about yesterday, we'd probably put up a big fight. Yet when the
stranger turns out to be us, we wallow in the past wantonly. We seldom try to stop ourselves.

Staying mired in the past is self-inhibiting. And it's not as if we
haven't heard the warnings against it: Don't cry over spilled milk.
What's done is done. Forgive and forget. And who among us doesn't
have at least one copy (I have five, plastered wherever there's an
empty space) of what could be called the Worrywart's Prayer, but is
actually known as "The Serenity Prayer"? This prayer hits the bull's-
eye squarely when it asks God to grant us serenity to "accept the
things [we] cannot change, courage to change the things [we] can,
and [develop] the wisdom to know the difference." Sound advice.
Too bad we have such trouble processing it.

The past is something we cannot change. It's kaput, over, done with, finito, and the smart way of dealing with it is to accept it, learn from it, then drop it like a hot poker. Otherwise, it can hold us captive for hours or even days, as our thoughts pull up a chair with worry, guilt, regret and their sisters, "I should have done this" and "I should have done that," and have a grand time gabbing about what might have been. And while this party continues long after we can gain any lesson from it, we lose out, as all the good things God has planned for us in the present slip by unnoticed, without so much as a how-do-you-do.

The Bible says each man's "life is but a breath," and that God has "decided the length of our lives . . . how many months we will live . . ." So we have to ask ourselves: "How much of it can we afford to spend on a past we can't do anything about?" and "When do we cut our losses, get out of town and, most important, never look back?" My guess is as little as possible, and as soon as possible. Lot's wife didn't, and we all know what happened to her.

What's more, if we believe, as the Bible tells us, that these days are "determined," "ordained" and "written in [God's] book before one of them came to be," then everything in the past, despite how we feel about it, is exactly what was supposed to have happened. This unique mix of experiences, both good and bad, is what makes us who we are today, and who we'll be tomorrow. So worrying about them is not only a time waster, but also a bit like questioning God's plan, which we know from some rather stern comments God made to Job from the whirlwind ("Are you trying to put me in the wrong and yourself in the right?") does not make him happy.

Most of the time, what we worry about isn't worth a hill of beans anyway. A woman we'll call Victoria, for instance, admitted she stewed two weeks about a fight she had had with her husband. She had conversations with people, went places and had meals she couldn't tell you a thing about because she spent most of her time in the past going over every detail of the incident. Meanwhile, when she finally brought the subject up again, she said her husband couldn't believe she'd been in such turmoil over something he'd forgotten the afternoon it happened.

God's like Victoria's husband in that respect. He doesn't hold our sins against us.

As soon as we confess, ask his forgiveness, and steel our wills to change, the past is past. He doesn't want us to wallow in guilt and worry. The Bible says, "If a wicked person . . . begins to obey my laws and do what is just and right . . . all his past sins will be forgotten." After all, what good is served by continuously rewinding and playing the tape of our wrongdoings anyway?

Still, letting go of the past requires a really concerted effort, even for stalwarts like Paul. "I am still not all I should be," he writes in his letter to the Philippians, then adds with determination, "but I am bringing all my energies to bear on this one thing: Forgetting the past and looking forward to what lies ahead." Paul says he's doing this—resolving to look ahead instead of looking back—"because of what Christ Jesus did for us." If we resolve to do that, too, we'll have an easier time of it, because if we keep our minds occupied with Jesus, there'll be no room for worrisome thoughts of the past.

PRAYER

Dearest Jesus,

I spent too much time yesterday in the past. It happens a lot. I go over and over things people say or do; things I say or do. Meantime, I'm leaving all the little gifts you've left for me in the present unopened. Not too smart. With your help, though, and more effort on my part, I'm determined to stop wasting time. Lord, give me the grace to chase the past back to where it belongs so it doesn't interfere with my today. And help me to be focused, like Paul, forward.

◆ ◆ ◆

CHAPTER 32

Criticism

Public opinion is a weak tyrant compared with our own private opinion. What a man thinks of himself— that is what determines his fate.

—HENRY DAVID THOREAU

I think fatuous praise from a manifest fool may hurt more than any depreciation.

—C. S. LEWIS

If the world hates you, keep in mind that it hated me first.

—JOHN 15:18

Don't grumble about each other, brothers. Are you
yourselves above criticism? For see! The great Judge is
coming. . . . Let Him do whatever criticizing must be done.

—JAMES 5:9 TLB

Do what is right; then if men speak against you, calling
you evil names, they will become ashamed of themselves for
falsely accusing you when you have only done what is good.

—1 PETER 3:16 TLB

Don't criticize, and then you won't be criticized.

—MATTHEW 7:1 TLB

If Jesus had a drachma for everyone who criticized him, he probably could have bought dinner for the five thousand people who
heard him preach on the mount and still have money left over.

Everywhere he went, people were critical of him for everything
from eating with tax collectors to curing sick people on the Sabbath,
from telling a cripple his sins were forgiven to refusing to lie about
who he was. Even when he was dying, the criminal next to him
denounced him for not coming down from the cross and saving
them both.

Yet criticism never worried him. He never got flustered or
stamped his feet and said, "Who do they think they are?" He never

pouted or felt downtrodden. He didn't harbor vengeful thoughts or call his critics names. He knew criticism came with the territory, that certain people would not understand him, reject him and be jealous of him. But he wasn't out for the popular vote. He was never a people pleaser. "Don't imagine that I came to bring peace," he said. And that included peace for himself. Lots of people weren't happy with his message or his methods. But he expected that. He didn't bow or become a slave to other people's opinions.

As followers of Christ, we have to walk in his shoes. So we, too, have to expect people will take shots at our beliefs. Folks will say we're silly to go to church, wasting money if we give to the poor, a fool if we don't cheat on our taxes, a prude if we don't like baseless sex in movies. They'll criticize us directly or say nasty things about the church or church officials. "In fact," Paul told Timothy, "everyone who wants to live a godly life in Christ Jesus will be persecuted." We can't stop rebukes from coming. If we wear the bulletproof vest of faith, these barbs can strike us, but they can't hurt us.

Lots of times, unwarranted criticism is just veiled jealousy. People are envious of us for one reason or another, and to ease their own insecurities, they knock us about something, totally out of left field. Take Moses, for example. He finally gets himself a wife, and his sister and brother do nothing but kvetch. "A Cushite woman?" Miriam complains to Aaron. Moses's siblings picked on him for this choice. But they probably wouldn't have cared if he had married an Irish Catholic from the Bronx. What was really bothering them was the fact that Moses had an in with God to the point where he spoke with him face-to-face and they didn't.

God saw through the whole incident and called Miriam and Aaron on the carpet for what they said. And the results weren't pretty. (See Numbers, chapter 12.) God will certainly deal with people who criticize us out of envy as well. But in the meantime, the Bible says the best thing we can do is grin and prayer it. "Don't snap back at those who say unkind things about you," says Peter. "Instead, pray for God's help for them . . . and God will bless you for it."

If we do what we believe in our hearts to be right, we shouldn't worry about the opinion of others. And though folks may talk about us, we know Jesus will be the ultimate judge. "Why are you criticizing her?" he asked his disciples when a woman poured expensive perfume on his feet. They were all too ready to chastise her for wasting money. But Jesus had the last word. "She has done a good thing to me. And she will always be remembered for this deed." He will remember our faith under fire as well.

P.S.: Obviously, since none of us is perfect, valid criticism can be a valuable tool. And though we might not want to hear it, the Bible warns us about thinking we're above it. "If you refuse [valid] criticism, you will end up in poverty and disgrace," advises Proverbs. So why not accept it and get all the help you can? Moreover, though it may be less to our liking, the Bible says criticism is preferable in some cases. "It is better," Ecclesiastes says, "to heed a wise man's rebuke than to listen to the song of fools." So rather than worrying when someone criticizes us good-naturedly, the smarter thing to do would be to pat him on the back and say, "Thanks for the tip."

PRAYER

Dearest Jesus,

Sometimes people make fun of me because of my beliefs. I get upset inside and either don't say anything or else I want to tell them off. Help me to have the faith and serenity to let them know calmly that being a Christian is no laughing matter. But if they continue, let me bear the brunt of their criticism as you did when people mocked you. On the other hand, when people criticize me for my own good, help me be humble enough to accept what they say and learn from the experience.

◆ ◆ ◆

CHAPTER 33

Terrorism

I trust in God's unfailing love forever and ever.

—PSALM 52:8 NLT

[He is] a faithful God who does no wrong.

—DEUTERONOMY 32:4

Yet, in the maddening maze of things,
And tossed by storm and flood,
To one fixed trust my spirit clings;
I know that God is good!

—JOHN GREENLEAF WHITTIER

God has made thee to love Him, and not to understand Him.

—VOLTAIRE

Will not the judge of all earth do right?

—GENESIS 18:25

I fear no foe with thee at hand to bless; Ills have
no weight, and tears no bitterness.

—HENRY FRANCIS LYTE

You have to give God the benefit of the doubt.

—SACHA GUITRY

God is our refuge and strength, an ever-present help in
trouble. Therefore we will not fear, though the earth give
way and the mountains fall into the heart of the sea.

—PSALM 46:1, 2

September 11 not only was a stab in the heart of anyone who
has ever loved, it was the end of life as we knew it—a fairy-
tale existence that viewed terrorism as something that happens on
the six o'clock news in other countries, or on the big screen in a

blockbuster summer movie. That bubble's burst now, replaced by a black cloud of grief, fear and anxiety. And if we never worried before, we're worrying now.

Yes, these days, even well-adjusted, logical, churchgoing people are nervous wrecks when it comes to boarding a plane, celebrating national holidays or gathering in a crowd. We feel trapped and impotent, at the mercy of madmen, wondering when and where these assassins will strike next. Worse than that, though, these tragedies, and the aftermath of constant anxiety left in their wake, have many of us shaken and questioning our faith.

And that's exactly where the terrorists want us. The Bible says, "Do not be afraid of those who kill the body but cannot kill the soul. Rather, be afraid of the One who can destroy both soul and body." Terrorists look to do just that. Using horrors like the Oklahoma bombing, 9/11 and the Chechnya massacre, they seek not only to kill and maim us, but also to drive a wedge between us and the only One who can see us through the carnage: our God.

Terrorists and the evil they propagate have us feeling like Job—abandoned and despondent, crying out in a loud voice to the heavens, "Why?" Job never did get an answer, but despite the death of his children, the loss of his wealth and the agony of pain and sickness, he would not walk away from the Lord. He would not, as his wife urged him, "curse God and die!" "Though he slay me," Job wailed, "yet will I trust him." In so doing, he passed the single most important test of his lifetime—that of accepting God's will under horrendous circumstances—a test that unbeknownst to him had cosmic repercussions, not just for him, but for all of mankind. Job proved that bad things can happen to good people—and those people can still cling to their core belief in a God who is good. "There is no truer statement than this," Job professed in the midst of his anguish. "God will not do wrong."

But other forces will. So, like Job, we must learn to stick with God, no matter what. Though our hearts are breaking, our spirits crushed and our level of anxiety is over the top, we have to hold fast to what we know, despite what we don't understand. We know that the God who sent his only Son to be nailed to a cross for us loves us and can only be a source of refuge through pain and suffering— never a source of blame. And we know that in his own time, he will answer all our cries for fairness, justice and an end to evil, just as certainly as he answered the suffering of Good Friday with the joy of Easter Sunday.

The Bible says, "[When people cry out for God's help] . . . He never replies by instant punishment of the tyrants. But it is false to say he doesn't hear those cries, and it is even more false to say he doesn't see what is going on. He *does* bring about justice at last if you will only wait."

While we wait, there are things we can do to avoid feeling trapped, afraid and powerless. Prayer is at the top of the list, followed by a firm commitment not to let anxieties about terrorism rob us of life, but instead make us more alive. It's something we can do for ourselves, all those who've died, and all those who grieve for them. So for them, let's take more joy in a sunny day and the smell of newly mown grass. Let's eat more ice cream and say less about the calories. Let's hug our children more and say "I love you" every time we say "good-bye." Let's smile more at people we don't know and not wait for a special occasion to buy a friend a gift. Let's sip more wine, dance more at weddings and spend more time listening to beautiful music. Let's live more fully and enjoy the things that those who have died would have, hoping their spirits are close by, drinking in the fullness.

PRAYER

Dearest Jesus,

There are a lot of things I don't understand—people blowing up other people is one of them. There's no sense to it. But I have to trust in the big picture of your Father's plan, just as you always did. And when I'm tempted to ask, "How can God let this happen?" or when I foolishly look for fairness and sanity in an unjust and insane universe, help me look to your cross and remember how God turned what the world did to you into our salvation.

◆ ◆ ◆

CHAPTER 34

Can You Hear Me Now? (Being Alone)

I will lie down in peace and sleep, for though I am alone, O LORD, you will keep me safe.

—PSALM 4:8 TLB

I never found the companion that was as companionable as solitude.

—HENRY DAVID THOREAU

. . . and lo, I am with you always, even unto the end of the age.

—MATTHEW 28:20 NKJV

At close of day, with God I walk, my garden's grateful shade;
I hear His voice among the trees, and I am not afraid.

—ANONYMOUS

The person who has not learned to be happy and content
while completely alone for an hour a day, or a week,
has missed life's greatest serenity.

—H. CLAY TATE

Do not be afraid, for I am with you.

—ISAIAH 43:5

God is always speaking to us, but the external
noise of the world and the internal churning of
our passions confuse us.

—FRANÇOIS FÉNELON

Whether we are high above the sky, or in the
deepest ocean, nothing in all creation will ever be
able to separate us from the love of God that is
revealed in Christ Jesus, our LORD.

—ROMANS 8:39 NLT

O ther than at Macy's without a credit card during a half-off sale of already-marked-down designer clothes, alone is a place we worrywarts hate to be. That's because, according to Merriam-Webster's, it means we're "separated from others," and we don't like the way that feels.

Separation anxiety doesn't just affect kindergarteners, and for many, the thought of spending any more time than we have to completely on our own pushes our panic buttons and stimulates our worrywart glands. We feel anxious, and we can't even explain why. We feel like frightened children, uneasy and insecure.

To avoid that dreaded state, we join organizations, attend meetings, take on extra work, surround ourselves with people we love and perfect strangers. In short, we fill up our lives' dance cards with all manner of distractions. Yet somehow, even in the din, we still feel alone. We're still left with an emptiness no one or nothing can seem to fill. And when, inevitably, the people in our lives move on, away, die or just plain don't keep in touch anymore, we feel abandoned again—empty and apart.

Meantime, Jesus, the one Being who can relieve the gnawing feeling of aloneness, is trying to break through, trying to make contact. "Can you hear me now?" he asks. "It's me, God. I'm here with you. And I love you," he assures us. "I can take away your fear and anxieties. I can fill the void if you'll let me."

Indeed, though people come and go in our lives, though we feel at times lonely, afraid and forsaken, Jesus promised us, "I am with you always." Even better, the Bible tells us nothing can separate us from him. So though our anxieties overwhelm us and make us lose sight of the fact, we need never worry about being alone—because the Antidote lies within us all the time. Jesus can meet and conquer our loneliness with his presence if we will only answer his call.

Ironically, once we do, we could find ourselves more separated from the world than ever before. When our connection with Jesus becomes clearer, instead of being anxious about being alone, we'll welcome our solitary moments. But the result will be less time for those people and distractions we once couldn't get enough of. And as our relationship with our Savior builds, people—even our loved ones and friends—may not understand, be sympathetic to or may even be offended by our change of heart.

Still, the pain of this loss is a small price to pay for the companionship of the Lord Jesus Christ. He will help us carry this cross as he knows full well how it feels to be cut off from everyone—his disciples (". . . all the disciples deserted him and fled"), and even for that awful, dark moment, by his Father ("My God, my God, why have you forsaken me?").

So let's stop running away from solitude. Let's embrace it, make time for it and use it as an opportunity to strengthen our connection to Jesus. Let's foster his companionship above all others and remember that with him by our sides, we may be alone, but we can never be lonely.

PRAYER

Dearest Jesus,

How can I expect to hear your call if I'm out of range trying to alleviate my sense of aloneness in the world's hullabaloo? Help me realize that only you can comfort me; only you can erase that empty feeling. Teach me, Lord, that the sooner I disconnect from the world, the sooner I'll feel connected to you.

◆　◆　◆

CHAPTER 35

Life—What a Pain

Surely he has borne our infirmaties and carried our diseases.

—ISAIAH 53:4 NRSV

In suffering, one learns to pray best of all.

—HAROLD A. BOSLEY

"Daughter," he said to her, "your faith has healed you. Go in peace."

—LUKE 8:48 TLB

Know how sublime a thing it is to suffer
and be strong.

—HENRY WADSWORTH LONGFELLOW

Our suffering is not worthy of the name of suffering.
When I consider my crosses, tribulations, and temptations,
I shame myself almost to death, thinking what they are
in comparison of the sufferings of my blessed
Savior Christ Jesus.

—MARTIN LUTHER

Physical pain however great ends in itself and falls
away like dry husks from the mind, whilst moral
discords and nervous horrors sear the soul.

—ALICE JAMES

Although the world is full of suffering, it is full
also of the overcoming of it.

—HELEN KELLER

No pain, no palm; no thorns, no throne; no gall,
no cross, no crown.

—WILLIAM PENN

God is our refuge and strength, an ever-present
help in trouble.

—PSALM 46:1

And whatever their illness and pain, or if they
were possessed by demons, or were insane, or paralyzed—
he healed them all.

—MATTHEW 4:24 TLB

Two middle-aged women sit next to each other in an HMO's
waiting room. One is constantly moving around in her seat,
sighing and muttering to herself.

"You seem a bit upset," says the second woman. "Is there anything
I can do? Maybe talking about it will help," she says gently.

"Oh, sorry, am I fidgeting?" says the first woman. "It's my back.
It's been acting up for months now. They take X-rays. They give me
pills. I go to therapy. And nothing helps. I just know I'll be an invalid
soon. I'm a nervous wreck thinking about it."

"That's awful. But, you shouldn't worry so much. It's not good for
you. In fact, it could be making matters worse."

"How so?"

"Well, you know, I read somewhere if you worry, you tense up.
Your muscles go all tight and that makes the pain worse."

"Really? But I can't help it."

"I understand," says the second woman, pushing a strand of stray hair to the side of her head. "It's hard not to worry when you're in pain. But, listen," she says, "do you mind if I make a suggestion? I mean, I'm sure your doctor is good and all. But I know a physician who can help you with the worry *and* the pain."

"Do you need a referral?"

"Nope, and he won't bounce you back and forth to a dozen different specialists either. He can cure you himself. He's handled all kinds of difficult cases—skin disease, internal bleeding, leg injuries, bad eyes. You name it. Really. I'm surprised you haven't heard of him. He's been written up everywhere—books, magazines, papers.

"And another thing," the second woman says, leaning in closer, "he takes time with you. He's not in a hurry. He listens to your symptoms, and he's extremely empathetic. I kind of get the impression he's been through a lot himself. And, you know, that's the best kind of doctor to have—one who's seen plenty of pain and knows firsthand what it's like. He won't slough it off, tell you it's all in your head or that you're overreacting."

"Does he accept Medicare?"

"Yup. And he makes house calls, too. Honest-to-goodness. And get this," the second woman continues, her eyes widening, "I heard he once cured a man without even seeing him . . . with just a word. A word, for Pete's sake! So if he can do all that, he can certainly help you with your back."

"And the worrying?" the first woman asks.

"And the worrying," the second woman replies. "Listen, he gave an outdoor seminar about anxiety once. Free! And would you believe he threw in a fish-and-chips lunch as well? People came from miles. I heard it was a mob scene. But anyway, the whole talk boiled down to this: worrying isn't healthy. It doesn't solve anything. It won't help you live a day longer. So don't worry. Of course, I'm over-simplifying here. He said it more eloquently, I'm sure. But, you know, you get the gist of it."

"I get it," says the first woman, closing the magazine she had open on her lap. "But this all sounds way out. It's just a little too good to be true. What's the gimmick? Is he one of those New Age guys? One of those faith healers?"

"No gimmick. But well, now that you mention it, I have to say he does have one prerequisite. You've got to trust him—completely. But what doctor doesn't expect that? I mean, if you don't believe your physician can help you, nothing he'll do for you is likely to make you better. Don't you agree?"

Before she could answer, though, the other woman continued.

"Look, all I'm saying is it can't hurt to try him. I know when I'm in pain, there's no one I'd rather go to. I can't imagine what I would have done without him. Oh, and another thing: I used to drive myself insane worrying. And well, to be honest with you, I still drive myself insane worrying . . . but not as often. So I'm improving. You know, a leopard can't change her spots overnight. But I'm a heck of a lot better than I was."

"Okay, okay," says the first woman, "You've convinced me. I'll give him a call. Can you write his name down for me? But before you do," she says, "I'm really curious about something. Can I ask you a question?"

"Sure, anything."

"If this other doctor is so wonderful, and you've had such great success with him, what in the world are you doing here?"

"It's my son's birthday," says the second woman. "I'm taking him to lunch." And with that, she starts to get up as a tall young man with a stethoscope around his neck walks into the reception area.

"Don't forget to give me that name," the first woman says.

"I'll do one better," she said, reaching into her purse. "Here's his card."

"Thanks so much," says the first woman, slipping the card into her pocket. "Nice talking with you."

"Mom?" asks the son, smiling, as they walked away. "Have you been giving out those cards again?"

"Guilty as charged," the woman says. "Ever heard of a second opinion? Well, I just gave her mine. That's all."

When they were out of sight, the first woman took the card out and looked at it. It read:

Jesus Christ, Divine Healer
Aches, Pains, Worries, Surgery
Believe in Him and Your Faith
Will Make You Whole.

PRAYER

Dearest Jesus,

There is no one who knows more about pain and suffering than you. You experienced the worst anyone could. Just thinking about it made you sweat blood. You even asked your Father to let the cup pass . . . it was that awful. Yet, you took it all on . . . to wipe my slate clean. Help me to keep this visual picture in my head when I'm tempted to complain about my paltry aches and pains. And when I face more serious illnesses, be with me in my suffering, help me be patient through it and if it be your will, heal me, as you have so many times before.

◆ ◆ ◆

CHAPTER 36

God Is My Sleeping Pill

The sovereign cure for worry is prayer.

—WILLIAM JAMES

Let prayer be the key of the day and the bolt of the night.

—JEAN PAUL RICHTER

You are safe in the care of the Lord your God,
just as though you were safe inside his purse!

—1 SAMUEL 25:29 TLB

A man who says his prayers in the evening is a captain
posting his sentries. After that, he can sleep.

—CHARLES BAUDELAIRE

The whole burden of the whole life of every
man may be rolled on to God.

—HENRY WARD BEECHER

You will not be afraid when you go to bed,
and you will sleep soundly through the night.
You will not have to worry. . . .
The LORD will keep you safe.

—PROVERBS 3:24–26 TEV

The exercise of prayer . . . must be regarded as the
most adequate and normal of all the pacifiers of
the mind and calmers of the nerves.

—DR. THOMAS HYSLOP

He lifts the burdens from those bent down
beneath their loads.

—PSALM 146:8 TLB

Since we can't turn our minds off like we turn off the lights, worrywarts are at their most vulnerable at nighttime. Lying in bed, our thoughts free to wander, we inevitably get stuck in a round robin of should-haves, what-ifs and what-am-I-going-to-dos, while the morning alarm looms closer and our bodies beg us to shut down and get some rest. Then, adding insult to injury, we pile on additional worries because we're not getting the sleep we need and will wind up feeling like zombies in the morning.

There's a sure cure for nights like this—prayer—and it can work better than the strongest sleeping pill if we can only surrender to its calming effects. Let's back up and look at why.

When we worry, what's actually happening is that we're having a negative conversation with ourselves about ourselves, and we're getting nowhere. This revs us up, keeps our minds agitated and holds our thoughts captive in turmoil—which is not exactly conducive to a sound night's sleep. On the other hand, when we pray, we're talking to someone outside ourselves—the Almighty God—who can do all things, not the least of which is helping us use nighttime for what he created it for: sleep.

The Bible says, "Don't worry about anything; instead, pray about everything; tell God your needs, and don't forget to thank Him. . . . If you do this, you will experience God's peace, which is far more wonderful than the human mind can understand, a peace which will keep your thoughts and your hearts quiet and at rest in Christ Jesus." So it stands to reason that if we can substitute prayer for worry, we can disconnect from our own restless selves and plug in to God, who can spread his serenity over us faster than we can say "Rip Van Winkle."

Still, trotting out our entire list of anxieties and praying over them point by point with God might not be the best course of action at 2 A.M. In fact, that would only get us obsessing about them again. A simple, heartfelt prayer would be better. Something like, "Father, I'm exhausted. I'm all wound up and I need help. Your Word tells us to 'give our burdens over to the Lord. He will carry them.' So I'd like to take you up on the offer. Please hold my worries for the night so I can get some sleep. Thank you, Lord. Amen." While we're at it, we might also ask him to infuse us with the grace we need to put more faith in his will and less in our own, so we can avoid our anxieties keeping us up at night in the first place. We might also try thanking God for all the fantastic things he gave us during the day (also known as counting our blessings). But by then, we'll probably already be asleep.

PRAYER

Dearest God,

You created the night for resting—not for worrying. Yet I can't, as the Bible suggests, "lie down without fear and enjoy pleasant dreams," while I stew about problems at the office, my husband's health or how we're going to afford a trip to Ireland and a snowblower. So, Lord, help me take my mind off myself and focus it on you. Help me, Lord, open my mind to the peace you offer so I can get some sleep, put more trust in you so dumb things like this don't keep me up and always be grateful for the gift of rest you offer.

◆ ◆ ◆

CHAPTER 37

Testing 1, 2, 3

These trials are only to test your faith, to see whether
or not it is strong and pure. It is being tested as fire tests
gold and purifies it—and your faith is far more precious to
God than mere gold; so if your faith remains strong after
being tried in the test tube of fiery trials, it will bring you
much praise and glory and honor on the day of his return.

—1 PETER 1:7 TLB

But he knows where I am going. And when he has tested
me like gold in a fire, he will pronounce me innocent.

—JOB 23:10 NLT

For when your faith is tested, your endurance has
a chance to grow. So let it grow, for when your endurance
is fully developed, you will be strong in character and
ready for anything.

—JAMES 1:3, 4 NLT

Happy is the man who doesn't give in and do wrong
when he is tempted, for afterwards he will get as his
reward the crown of life that God has promised those
who love him.

—JAMES 1:12 TLB

Do you remember how the Lord led you through the
wilderness for all those forty years, humbling you and
testing you to find out how you would respond, and
whether or not you would really obey him? Yes, he
humbled you by letting you go hungry and then feeding
you with manna. . . . He did it to help you realize that
food isn't everything, and that real life comes by
obeying every command of God.

—DEUTERONOMY 8:2, 3 TLB

Tests give us the willies. They make our palms sweat and our brows furrow, yet they're a necessary slice of the pie we call life. Among other things, they help us evaluate and certify our knowledge, find out if we're healthy or sick, and assess our strength and mental stability in times of difficulty or stress. What's more, if we crack open the Bible, we'll find that God uses tests big-time to build the one thing he requires of us all: faith.

Take Noah, for example. God told him he was going to "put an end to all people," an anxiety-ridden statement if ever there was one. But in the same breath, God also told him, "I will establish my covenant with you." So when God told Noah to build a huge boat, put his family and animals on it and get ready for the floodwaters, Noah didn't bat an eyelash. God's promise was enough for him. So he "obeyed God," and "by his faith," the Bible says, "was made right in God's sight," not to mention saving himself, his whole family and the world in the bargain. In other words, Noah aced his test.

God tested Abraham, too. And though there were a few glitches (leaving Canaan for Egypt, duping Pharaoh about his wife and not letting go of his nephew, Lot), overall Abraham's faith got high marks. For instance, when God told him to go to another land, the Bible says, Abraham packed up and "away he went, not even knowing where he was going." When God told him to circumcise every male in his family, that's exactly what he did. When God told him his descendants would be countless like the stars (despite some initial skepticism), the Bible says, "Abram believed the LORD," and "God considered him righteous on account of his faith." Then, of course, when it came to the hardest test of all, Abraham's faith literally shone as he was "willing to obey God, even if it meant offering his son, Isaac, to die on the altar."

And the list goes on. Joseph, Moses, the Israelites, Joshua, David, Daniel, Shadrach, Meshach, Abednego, Job, Jonah, Mary, Joseph, Peter, Paul—God tested them all, and they passed with flying colors.

How'd they do it? The Bible says they made their decisions by "faith." In other words, they hadn't a clue why things were going as they were, why there was this setback and that. But they were willing to give the Almighty his due, acknowledge that, as the Supreme Being, he had everything under control. So they took him at his word, and obeyed him despite the circumstances. They had faith that God was powerful, loving and trustworthy enough to see them through any trial that came their way. And that's exactly what God did.

That's why testing is so important. It gives us a chance to increase the "measure of faith" God gives us all. It provides us with the opportunity to shine in God's eyes, to please him and demonstrate our love. It shows God we are willing to trust him not only when things are going great, but when we lose a job, a husband, a home, when disasters strike and nothing makes sense. And each time we pass one of these tests, we gain experience. Each time we place our trust in God, not knowing the outcome, we're emboldened, and that strengthens our faith even more.

Where does worry fit into all of this? It doesn't. Because we can't face trials or solve problems—we can't grow stronger in faith and get closer to God if we're stuck in worry. Anxiety clouds our minds, makes us indecisive and unsure. And "whoever doubts," the Bible tells us, "is like a wave in the sea that is driven and blown about by the wind." And how can we prove our faith in that state? Indeed, worrying keeps us trying to reason and find answers to things that we can't understand. It confuses, frustrates and holds us back. In a nutshell, worrying sets us up for failure.

And it's so unnecessary because we have God's promise that nothing that comes our way will be insurmountable. How can it be if we have God's power inside of us? What's more, we have his promise that he will never raise the bar so high we can't jump it. The Bible says, "God keeps his promise, and he will not allow you to be tested beyond your power to remain firm; at the time you are put to the test, he will give you the strength to endure it, and so provide you with a way out." That's because God knows us. He knows our limits. He knows what we can and can't do. So he custom-designs each test especially for us.

And if our faith falters again? Well, there's still nothing to get anxious about because God doesn't give up if we don't. The Bible says, "even when we are too weak to have any faith left, he remains faithful to us and will help us, for he cannot disown us who are part of himself. . . ." So he may take us around again and again. Then he may take us around one more time. Rest assured, though, he will never flunk us as long as we keep on trying.

PRAYER

Dearest Jesus,

"O, you of little faith" certainly describes me. Because no matter how many times you bail me out of trouble, sickness and desperation, when trials surface again, I still get anxious. So I thank you, Lord, for being so patient with me. I praise you for not giving up on me. And I ask you to continue to send me little and big tests so I can work on my faith. Help me recognize these trials are not meant to drag me down, but rather to build me up, and that however impossible or painful they may appear at the outset, they will always result in my ultimate good. Give me the strength to stop worrying so that I can increase my faith and show you that though I am weak, my love for you is strong.

◆　◆　◆

CHAPTER 38

Addicted to Worry

People with no regard for others can throw whole cities into turmoil. Those who are wise keep things calm.

—PROVERBS 29:8 TEV

Don't worry about anything; instead pray about everything. ... If you do this, you will experience God's peace, which is far more wonderful than the human mind can understand. His peace will keep your thoughts and your hearts quiet and at rest as you trust in Christ Jesus.

—PHILIPPIANS 4:6, 7 TLB

Therefore having been justified by faith, we have peace
with God through our LORD Jesus Christ. . . .

—ROMANS 5:1 NRSV

But all who listen to me will live in peace and safety,
unafraid of harm.

—PROVERBS 1:33 NLT

A dry crust eaten in peace is better than a
great feast with strife.

—PROVERBS 17:1 NLT

"Eternal peace was within your reach and you turned
it down," (Jesus) wept, "and now it is too late."

—LUKE 19:42 TLB

There are no twelve-step programs for worriers. But I think
someone should start one, because chronic anxious behavior,
and the distress it causes both the worriers and those around them,
can be just as destroying as any hard-core addiction. Here's how one
woman explains it:

"I hated what worrying did to me. But I was addicted to the rush,"
explains Maria L, "and before I knew it, I couldn't control myself.

Now that I'm seeking help for my problem, I can see how intensely it affected me—not just emotionally—but physically as well. Worrying got me all revved up, like a blast of adrenaline. My heart began to pound; my pulse began to race and thoughts would stampede though my head like a herd of wild horses. I'd fixate on one bogus crisis after another all day. Somehow I felt more alive when I was worrying. It was almost as though I went out of my way to seek out things to be anxious about, as though I wasn't happy unless I was worrying."

Maria's life became a roller-coaster ride she willingly paid for with her serenity. Even worse, she says, is what her worrying did to the people around her. "I not only made my own life miserable, but sucked in my husband, daughters, neighbors, friends, anyone who would listen. It got so bad, nobody wanted to talk to me." Because she consistently got herself in a tizzy about so many situations, she says, when something genuinely worrisome did happen, à la "The Boy Who Cried Wolf," no one believed her.

Okay, so most of us aren't in Maria's league . . . yet. And we never have to be if we get closer to Jesus, because as the Bible explains, "Christ himself is our way of peace."

The Bible says Jesus is the "Prince of Prince," and with him we can get calm and stay peaceful—under any circumstances. "Peace is what I leave with you," Jesus said to his disciples. "It is my *own* peace that I give you," and we can be sure that when Jesus offers us peace, it's not like any other we've ever known.

Certainly, there are times when we seem at peace when everything is going hunky-dory and the world is our oyster. But then, inevitably, something happens, our minds get caught up in worry, and we become anxious and fearful again. But the last part of Jesus's promise to us is that the peace he offers "isn't fragile" like the kind the world gives. In other words, the peace Jesus left us with isn't temporary, like the lulling feelings of false security we get from relationships, money, good health or a nice home—feelings that are fleeting and dependent on things that can change in a heartbeat.

The peace Jesus offers isn't tied to a thing. It's tied to him. So it's everlasting. What's more, it's all encompassing and it's powerful—strong enough to conquer the pull of anxiety. Best of all, though, it's there for us anytime, even smack in the middle of a crisis.

Jesus paid for this gift with his blood. The Bible says, "He was wounded and bruised for our sins. He was beaten that we might have peace; he was lashed—and we were healed!" Through his suffering, he made "peace" with the Father in our name. So we are back in God's good graces with the knowledge that nothing can ever separate us and nothing has the power to ruffle us—unless we let it.

The Bible says we can have "real peace with God because of what Jesus Christ our Lord has done for us," and that God promises to "keep in perfect peace all those who trust in him, whose thoughts turn often to the Lord." So if we concentrate on Jesus, praying and talking to him often, instead of brewing up imaginary problems, we'll go through our days with an inner sense of harmony that won't require a jolt of worry to make us feel alive.

Jesus knows that being in a constant state of turmoil is no fun. That's why he encourages us to kick the worry habit. "Do not be worried," he tells us. "Do not be afraid," he says. So let's open and use the gift of peace he gave us. With it, we can stop looking for trouble, live a more harmonious life, and have more time and energy to enjoy the goodness he has planned for us. The Bible says, "God wants his children to live in peace and harmony." So let's start doing just that today.

PRAYER

Dearest Jesus,

I want to be my own disaster master. I want to stop running from one imaginary crisis to another. I want to live a calm life when things are good, as well as when they're not so good. I know I can do this because your cross made it possible. Help me, Lord, to withdraw from worry and draw closer to you.

◆ ◆ ◆

CHAPTER 39

Death: The Ultimate Worry

The righteous hath hope in his death.

—PROVERBS 14:32 KJV

The last enemy to be destroyed is death.

—1 CORINTHIANS 15:26

The fear of death is worse than death.

—ROBERT BURTON

Death is the opening of a more subtle life.
In the flower, it sets free the perfume; in the chrysalis,
the butterfly; in man, the soul.

—JULIETTE ADAM

Death's but a path that must be trod, if man
would ever pass to God.

—THOMAS PARNELL

Be of good cheer about death, and know this of
a truth, that no evil can happen to a good man,
either in life or after death.

—SOCRATES

It is impossible that anything so natural, so necessary,
and so universal as death should ever have been
designed by Providence as an evil to mankind.

—JONATHAN SWIFT

We picture death as coming to destroy; let us rather picture
Christ as coming to save. We think of death as ending; let us
rather think of life as beginning, and that more abundantly.…
We think of going away; let us think of arriving.

—NORMAN MACLEOD

I have two words to say to worrywarts who fear death so much that they can't enjoy life: Merry Christmas. These words offer hope to a once hopeless world because through the miracle of Christmas, God has arranged it so that no one has to be afraid to die anymore. The Bible says, "God so loved the world that he gave his only begotten son, that whoever believes in him should not perish but have everlasting life."

But let's examine how death fits into the picture in the first place. "Death came into the world," the Bible says, "because of what one man [Adam] did, and it is because of what this other man [Christ] has done that now there is the resurrection from the dead."

In essence, by coming back from the grave, Christ rendered death moot. It was set in motion by sin, and that couldn't change. But because Christ rose, we now know death is not final. It no longer has a hold on us. It can't hurt us anymore. It's lost its "sting." Our Savior, Jesus, has vanquished death, and the Bible affirms the good news. Isaiah tells us the Lord "will swallow up death forever." David says God "has delivered my soul from death." John says, "God did not send his Son into the world to condemn it, but to save it." Jesus himself says, "Don't be afraid. I am the living one! I was dead, but now I am alive forever and ever. I have authority over death." Paul says, "He has ended the power of death, and through the gospel has revealed immortal life," but probably spells it out best for us worrywarts by explaining that Jesus "became flesh and blood . . . for only as a human being could he die and in dying break the power of the devil who had the power of death," and "in this way set free those who were slaves all their lives because of their fear of death."

The scary part for most of us isn't so much the dying, but what comes afterward: final judgment. Our sins make us fear and tremble at the thought of the Almighty. And that's the worry that Jesus has done away with. By coming to earth and suffering for us, Jesus has removed the fear because he's removed the sin. Jesus stood in for us, was judged and paid our debt, and God accepted his offering. In that magnanimous effort, our sin slates were wiped clean, and our ability to say "no" to sin and (spiritual) death was secured.

So if we accept Jesus, following his word as best we can and begging his forgiveness when we fail, we have no reason to fear God's wrath—and can stand before him without quaking. We have Jesus's promise on that: "I assure you," he tells us, "those who listen to my message and believe in God who sent me have eternal life. They will never be condemned for their sins, but they have already passed from death into life."

As if that weren't good news enough, there's more. Because our old sinful selves were joined with Jesus and died with him, they will also rise with him. "For I will live again," Jesus explained, "and you will, too."

Okay, but that doesn't mean the bodies we're in now won't go the way of all flesh. On the contrary, we are temporary people. We are destined to expire. The Bible says, "Yet, even though Christ lives within you, your body will die because of sin; but your spirit will live, for Christ has pardoned it." So it's as though we get rid of our outer casings, which were dust in the first place and will decompose back to dust and free up the other part of us, our spirits, to be joined to the new, improved bodies Paul tells us about. Actually, Paul says that getting rid of these earthly bodies is a prerequisite to getting into heaven. He says, "These perishable bodies of ours are not the right kind to live forever." And if that's the case, why anguish about letting them go?

Indeed, because of God's immense love for us, and what happened in that stable long ago, we don't have to agonize over losing our bodies or our souls. "We will not be ashamed and embarrassed at the day of judgment," the Bible says, "but can face him with confidence and joy because he loves us. . . . What's more, "His perfect love for us eliminates all dread of what he might do to us." So we can take death—and for that matter, the struggles and pain of life—off our worry lists for good. We no longer have to behave like "cowering, fearful slaves," anxious about living and petrified of dying, because Jesus gives us the strength to survive one and has broken the bond of the other. So let's exchange fear and terror for faith and hope. Let's rejoice in what Christ's birth and death accomplished. And let's never stop thanking God for the gift of Jesus, because as the choirs and carolers remind us each year in their hymns of praise, "Man will live forever more because of Christmas day."

PRAYER

Dearest Jesus,

The world has taught me well not to think about death, when, in fact, that's exactly what I should be focusing on. I should think about death every day, and while I'm at it, use the opportunity to jump up and down, bang pots and praise you for saving me from its grips. Okay, so banging pots might not always be feasible, but praising you certainly is. So that's what I'm going to do, starting this minute. "All honor and praise to you, Lord Jesus, forever and ever. You have taken the fear out of dying and given us hope for living. For this and for always being so good to me, I thank you, Amen."

◆ ◆ ◆

CHAPTER 40

It's Only Money

Charge them that are rich in this world, that they be not highminded, nor trust in uncertain riches, but in the living God, who giveth us richly all things to enjoy.

—1 TIMOTHY 6:17 KJV

Do good with what thou hast or it will do thee no good.

—WILLIAM PENN

When I have money, I get rid of it as quickly as possible, lest it find a way into my heart.

—JOHN WESLEY

There are no pockets in a shroud.

—ANONYMOUS

It's not what you'd do with a million,
if riches should e'er be your lot,
But what are you doing at present
with the dollar and a quarter you've got.

—ANONYMOUS

The true disciple of Jesus is neither a miser nor
a spendthrift, but a steward.

—WILLIAM HIRAM FOULDES

If the prize patrol ever came to my door with a gigantic check, I'd pretend I wasn't home. Okay, so maybe I *would* let them in, take the money and, in deference to my hardworking husband, use a bit to pay off the mortgage. But that's it. The rest would go to form a foundation: The Allia Nolan You-Can't-Take-It-With-You Foundation. I would be its CCG (Chief Cheerful Giver), and I'd spend my time dispensing envelopes of money, no strings attached, every day from nine to five.

Crazy? Nope. Altruistic? Nope. Fact is, I'd be using just plain common sense. I can take a warning, see, and that's just what Scripture is full of: wisdom cautioning us about the evils of a bulging wallet. I read enough of them to make my eyes sore, and I get the picture. Money is not to be trusted. It's an anxiety magnet. It's a wolf in sheep's clothing. It can't buy me anything really worthwhile, like a lovely seat in heaven next to my favorite biblical hero, Esther. But it *can* threaten my chances of getting to heaven at all. In short, money is dangerous and really just more trouble than it's worth.

We've all seen what money can do. It gives folks a swelled head. Once they're flush, people tend to sit around in nice homes, eating grapes and perusing bank books, all the while thinking it was their cleverness—and not the Lord—who gave them "power to become rich." Ecclesiastes, in particular, says money is addictive, not satisfying, and no matter how much a person has, it's never enough, not to mention it could get stolen or lost in an investment gone sour. Even worse, it says (and I paraphrase), a person can store up Swiss banks full of money anticipating one heck of a retirement, then die before he gets the chance to use it. Proverbs' prophesy is just as bad. It says "do not wear yourself out trying to get rich," because money tends to "fly off to the sky like an eagle," which would be just my luck, if I did happen onto a fortune and grew to like having it.

Money didn't hold much weight with Jesus or Paul. Jesus said, "Woe to you who are rich," and Paul called money "the root of all kinds of evil." No offense to the wealthy intended. But all these references lead me to believe that having big bucks makes it harder for people to get to heaven. And I'm already having problems. So when Jesus says, "It is easier for a camel to go through the eye of a needle than for a rich person to enter the kingdom of heaven," I'm all ears.

Money is not my friend. Why add another worry to my legion? Why complicate matters with "mammon"?

In its defense, with a helping of love, money can do a lot of good. It can save lives, rebuild countries and help researchers find cures to disease. But even a pinch of greed can spoil the mix. And *that* recipe winds up increasing hatred, death and destruction, as it makes enemies out of friends and tears families and countries apart. In my mind, money's just too treacherous.

So, I say, keep your sweepstakes and your scratch-and-wins. They're too risky. I'm okay with (and grateful to God for) what I have: more than enough to buy my daily bread, a bottle of wine now and again, and some sandals I don't really need from Payless. In fact, for my money, I think the best place to be when it comes to finances is not on top, but in the middle, a reason to pray the prayer of the Proverbs and ask God to give me "neither poverty nor riches."

That's why if I happened on to big money, I'd take what I needed to get by, and as Jesus told the wealthy man to do, give the rest to the poor. This way, I'd be storing up riches in heaven, where, my husband will be happy to know, I'll be getting the maximum interest. I do this with the utmost aplomb since, when it comes to investing in the future, I've got it on good word that God gives a much better return than mammon.

PRAYER

Dear God,

Through your grace, I've never known real poverty. I've always had what you promised to give me: enough to get by on. And more recently, some extra. So thank you, Lord, for the riches you've sent my way. I pray that I'll always recognize everything I have is through your generosity, and that it's my duty to share any windfall that may come my way with others not as fortunate. Help me be a cheerful giver, who offers freely, without fanfare and without expectation of return. Help me also recognize the power of money to do both good and evil, so that I can put the resources you give me to the best possible use.

◆   ◆   ◆

NOTES

3. Relaxing Without Guilt

Dale Carnegie, *How to Stop Worrying and Start Living* (New York: Simon & Schuster, 1984), 61.

"Come with me": Mark 6:31

4. Ten Pounds of Flesh

"I tell you": Matthew 6:25

5. Minding Today's Business

M. Scott Peck, *Further Along the Road Less Traveled* (New York: Simon & Schuster, 1978), 69.

"worry about tomorrow": Matthew 6:34 NLT (paraphrased)

Dale Carnegie, *How to Stop Worrying and Start Living* (New York: Simon & Schuster, 1984), quoting Dr. William Osler, 5.

6. Fortuitous Failure

"I will abandon my people": Hosea 5:15 TEV

"Let's return to the LORD": Hosea 6:1 TEV

"a righteous man": Proverbs 24:16 NKJV

"I have sinned before": 2 Samuel 12:13 TEV

"Peter went out": Matthew 26:75 TEV

"The Lord will make you go": Isaiah 30:20 TEV

"brings God's approval": Romans 5:4 TEV

"Happy is the person who": James 1:12 TEV

8. Chasing After Time

"It is not for you to know": Acts 1:7 NKJV (paraphrased)

"is in your hands": Psalm 31:15

10. Finding a Mate

Evagrius Ponticus, from Chapters on Prayer, quoted in Barnard Bangley, comp., *Morning and Evening with the Spiritual Classics: 40 Days of Meditations* (Wheaton, Illinois: Harold Shaw Publishers 1999), Day 2-Evening.

11. Job Jitters

"Do not worry about": Matthew 6:34

"All really intelligent men recognize the moment is everything," Goethe

"No heaven can come": Fra Giovanni, from a letter to his friend, Countess Allagia Aldobrandeschi, Christmas Eve, 1513.

12. Fueling Anxiety with Negativity

"Hasten, O God": Psalm 70:1

13. Neat to a Fault

Marilyn Lashbrook, *Good, Better, Best: The Story of Mary and Martha* (Dallas: Roper Press, 1994), 26.

"Lord, don't you care": Luke 10:40 (emphasis mine)

"Martha, Martha": Luke 10:41

"Seek first his kingdom": Matthew 6:33

14. Who Stole My Body?

"because of the sound": Psalm 102:5 NKJV

"a tranquil heart": Proverbs 14:30 NASB

"a joyful heart makes": Proverbs 15:13 NASB

"think like a child": 1 Corinthians 13:11 NASB

"put childish ways behind me." 1 Corinthians 13:11

"to transfer our lowly bodies": Philippians 3:21

"Whoever loses his life": Matthew 16:25 TEV

15. Accepting Joy

"and the joy of the Lord shall fill you full": Isaiah 41:16 TLB

"and your joy will be complete": Deuteronomy 16:15

"came so that we may": John 10:10 AMP

"with good things": Psalm 103:5 TLB

"evil men give their children": Matthew 7:11 (paraphrased)

"No eye has seen": 1 Corinthians 2:9

"the world will make you": John 16:33 TEV

16. Loss

"in all their distress": Isaiah 63:9

"Come boldly to the throne": Hebrews 4:16 NLT

"Cast your burden upon": Psalm 55:22 NRSV

17. Change—The Worrywart's Friend

"the spirit of the Lord": 1 Samuel 10:6

"if any man be in": 2 Corinthians 5:17 NASB

"put off your old self": Ephesians 4:24

"you, too, must be patient." James 5:7–10 NLT

18. Don't Worry, Be Silly
"*become as little children*": Matthew 18:3

19. Possessive Possessions
"*Don't worry about*": Matthew 6:25–32 TLB

"*serve two masters*": Matthew 6:24

"*ask and it will be given to you*": Matthew 7:7

"*I know what it is*": Philippians 4:12, 13

20. Timing
St. Augustine, *The Confessions of St. Augustine* (New York: Barnes & Noble, 1999), 267.

"*bore a son to Abraham*": Genesis 21:1, 2

Philip Yancy, *Disappointment with God.* (Grand Rapids, MI: Zondervan, 1988), 237.

"*and the Lord loves us*": Numbers 14:8 TLB

"*The LORD leads them with a shout!*" Joel 2:11 NLT

"*everything is possible*": Matthew 19:26

"*Everything that happens*": Ecclesiastes 3:1 TEV

"*Whether you turn to the right*": Isaiah 30:21

21. A Sympathetic Ear
"*cast all your anxiety*": 1 Peter 5:7

"*approach the throne*": Hebrews 4:16

"*unfailing love*": Psalm 52:8 NLT

"*I no longer call you servants*": John 15:15 NLT

22. Limiting Others' Lives

"perfect love drives out fear": 1 John 4:18

"love is not selfish": 1 Corinthians 13:5 TEV

"is not irritable": ibid.

"always trusts": 1 Corinthians 13:7

"Jesus loved Lazarus": John 11:5 TEV

"very, very sick": John 11:3 TLB

"love one another as I have": John 13:34 NKJV

23. Angels Abounding

"guard you": Psalm 91:11

"no harm will befall you, no disaster will come": Psalm 91:10

"up in their hands. . . ." Psalm 91:12

"strike your foot against a stone": ibid.

"185,000 Assyrian troops": 2 Kings 19:35 TLB

"entertained angels without": Hebrews 13:2 TLB

24. Attitude of Gratitude

Jerome Irving Rodale, *The Synonym Finder* (Emmaus, PA: Rodale Press, 1978), 434.

"will not forsake": Hebrews 13:5 NKJV

"protect": Psalm 37:39 TEV

"guard": 2 Thessalonians 3:3 TLB

"give thanks": 1 Thessalonians 5:18

"his faithful love": Jeremiah 33:11 NLT

"give thanks to the LORD": 1 Chronicles 16:8 NLT

"remember the wonders": 1 Chronicles 16:12

"For how can I thank you enough": Jonah 2:9 TLB

"always give thanks": Ephesians 5:20 (emphasis mine) TEV

25. Prayer, Practice, Pretending

"I do have faith, but": Mark 9:24 TEV

"Faith itself if it is not accompanied": James 2:17 (emphasis mine)

"You see that a person": James 2:24 (emphasis mine)

"My power is made": 2 Corinthians 12:9

"We were under great": 2 Corinthians 1:8, 9

26. Real Success

"Be sure to do what": Galatians 6:4, 5 NLT

"Commit to the LORD whatever you do": Proverbs 16:3

"Whatever you do, work at it with": Colossians 3:23, 24 (emphasis mine)

27. Evil

"can do all things through Christ": Philippians 4:13 NKJV

28. Your Father Always Loves You

"nothing can ever separate": Romans 8:38 NLT

"long ago, even before he made the world": Ephesians 1:4, 5 NLT

"he remembers our utter weaknesses, for his": Psalm 136:23 TLB (paraphrased)

"unfailing love": Psalm 52:8

29. Reining In Imagination

Paraphrased from Father Anthony de Mello, Society of Jesus Satellite Retreat, We and God Spirituality Center, St. Louis, Missouri, 1989.

"father of lies": John 8:44

"native language": ibid.

"examine everything carefully and hold fast to": Thessalonians 5:21 NASB

30. Two Worrisome Words

"Truth stands the test of": Proverbs 12:19 TLB

"A good man's mind is": Proverbs 12:5 TLB

"Lies will get any man": Proverbs 12:13 TLB

"corrupts the whole person": James 3:6

"direct my footsteps": Psalm 119:133

"Say only 'Yes,'": Matthew 5:37 TEV

"If you are the Son of God": Matthew 4:3

"It is written": Matthew 4:4

31. What's Done Is Done

"accept the things": "The Serenity Prayer" by Reinhold Niebuhr

"each man's life is but a breath": Job 7:7

"decided the length": Job 14:5 NLT

"determined": Job 14:5

"ordained, written in your book": Psalm 139:16

"Are you trying to": Job 40:8 TEV

"If a wicked man": Ezekiel 18:21, 22 TLB

"I am still not all": Philippians 3:13 TLB

"because of what Christ": Philippians 3:14 TLB

32. Criticism

"Don't imagine that I came": Matthew 10:34 NLT

"In fact, everyone who wants to live": 2 Timothy 3:12

"Don't snap back at": 1 Peter 3:9 TLB

"Why are you criticizing her?": Matthew 26:10 TLB

"She has done a good thing": ibid.

"And she will always be remembered for this deed": Matthew 26:13 TLB

"If you refuse criticism": Proverbs 13:18 TLB

"It is better to heed a wise": Ecclesiastes 7:5

33. Terrorism

"Do not be afraid of": Matthew 10:28

"Curse God and die": Job 2:9

"Though He slay me": Job 13:15 NKJV

"There is no truer statement": Job 34:12 NLT

"[When people cry out for]": Job 35:12–14 TLB

34. Can You Hear Me Now?

"I am with you always": Matthew 28:20 TLB

"Not death, life, angels, demons": Romans 8:38 TLB

"all the disciples": Matthew 26:56 TLB

"My God, My God": Matthew 27:46 TLB

36. God Is My Sleeping Pill

"Don't worry about anything": Philippians 4:6–7 TLB

"Give your burdens over": Psalm 55:22 TLB

"lie down without fear": Psalm 3:5 NLT

37. Testing 1, 2, 3

"put an end to all people": Genesis 6:13

"I will establish my covenant": Genesis 6:18

"obeyed God": Hebrews 11:7 NLT

"by his faith he . . . was made": ibid.

"away he went": Hebrews 11:8 TLB

"Abram believed": Genesis 15:6 NLT

"God considered him": Genesis 15:6 TLB

"willing to obey God": James 2:21 TLB

"by faith": Hebrews 11:8 TEV

"Measure of faith": Romans 12:3

"And whoever doubts is like": James 1:6 TEV

"God keeps his promise": 1 Corinthians 10:13 TEV

"even when we are too weak to have": 2 Timothy 2:13 TLB

"O you of little faith": Matthew 6:30

38. Addicted to Worry

"Christ himself": Ephesians 2:14 TLB

"Prince of Peace": Isaiah 9:6 TLB

"Peace is what I leave you": John 14:27 TEV (emphasis mine)

"It is my own peace I give you": ibid.

"isn't fragile": ibid. TLB

"He was wounded and bruised": Isaiah 53:5 TLB

"Peace with God through": Romans 5:1 TEV

"Keep in perfect peace": Isaiah 26:3 TLB

"Do not be worried . . . Do not be afraid": John 14:27 TEV

"God wants His children": 1 Corinthians 7:15 TLB

39. Death: The Ultimate Worry

"God so loved the world": John 3:16 NKJV

"Death came into the world": 1 Corinthians 15:21 TLB

"will swallow up death": Isaiah 25:8 TLB

"has delivered my soul": Psalm 56:13 NKJV

"God did not send His Son into the world": John 3:17 TLB

"Don't be afraid. . . . I am the living one!": Revelation 1:17, 18 TEV

"He has ended the power of death": 2 Timothy 1:10 TEV

"became flesh and blood": Hebrews 2:14 TLB

"in this way set free": Hebrews 2:15 TEV

"I assure you, those who listen to my message": John 5:24 NLT

"For I will live again, and you will too": John 14:19 NLT

"Yet, even though Christ lives within you": Romans 8:10 TLB

"These perishable bodies are not": 1 Corinthians 15:50 TLB

"We will not be ashamed and embarrassed": 1 John 4:17, 18 TLB

"cowering, fearful slaves": Romans 8:15 NLT

"man will live forevermore": from "Mary's Boy Child."

40. It's Only Money

". . . power to become rich": Deuteronomy 8:18 NLT

"addictive, not satisfying, never enough, stolen, die before using": Ecclesiastes 5:10–16
   NLT (paraphrased)

"wear yourselves out": Proverbs 23:4

"fly off to the sky like an eagle": Proverbs 23:5

"woe to you who are rich": Luke 6:24

"the root of all kinds of evil": 1 Timothy 6:10 NLT

"camel to go through the eye of a needle": Matthew 19:24 TEV

"neither poverty nor riches": Proverbs 30:8